LIVING LAN
of
FREEMASONRY

BARRY MITCHELL

Lewis Masonic

Dedication

The author would like to dedicate this collection of lectures to the memory of Alf Mann, with lasting thanks for his inspiration and encouragement.

Acknowledgement

The author would like to acknowledge the help of Reg Barrow, Curator of the Sussex Masonic Centre in providing the impetus to develop such a keen interest in Masonic history.

Front cover: Frontispiece of 1784 *Constitutions.*
The Library and Museum of Freemasonry, London

First published 2014

ISBN 978 0 85318 480 5

Published by Lewis Masonic

an imprint of Ian Allan Publishing Ltd, Hersham, Surrey KT12 4RG.

Printed in England

Visit the Lewis Masonic website at
www.lewismasonic.co.uk

CONTENTS

Illustrations

About the Author

Barry was born in South London during an air raid in 1943. He grew up just around the corner from John Major, with whom he used to play cricket in a local park. A varied adult career included working as a Laboratory Technician, teaching English in Germany and selling gramophone recordings to the BBC on behalf of Phillips Records. He then spent 27 years in sound broadcasting, but after 12 years attached to the BBC Arabic Service, he fell victim to Margaret Thatcher's instruction to the then Director General, John Birt to reduce staff levels and was given compulsory but generous retirement in 1992.

This was no ordinary retirement, no tea party, no ceremony, just 'Out!'. Two of his close friends committed suicide, and if it were not for a younger colleague who maintained contact, and appeared genuinely concerned for his welfare, a serious depression looked likely. He suggested that Barry might benefit from meeting a few new friends in London, who met regularly in a Tooley Street pub, which he did and was touched by the similar concern shown by apparent strangers. However, he was told that they were having a meeting upstairs, but he was welcome to pass the time with a newspaper and couple of pints of beer.

Next week the process was repeated and becoming curious, he asked one of them what they were doing. 'Rehearsing your Initiation' was the surprising answer. Freemasonry soon filled up his abundant spare time. His ultimate Masonic accolade however was being awarded the Freedom of the City of London, eventually becoming Centenary Master of the Guild of Freemen Mark Master Masons.

Masonic Achievements

Assistant Librarian, Sussex Masonic Centre, 1997-2003
Past Master – Zetland Lodge No. 511
Past Master – Servimus Lodge No. 5832
Past Master – Lignum Lodge No. 6744
Past Master – Hova Mark Lodge No. 168
MEZ Chapter of Light No. 7218
Past Sovereign – Blazing Star Chapter, Rose Croix No. 759
Centenary Master – Guild of Freemen Mark Lodge No. 647
Worshipful Master - Duke of Richmond Mark Lodge No. 1025

Introduction

Living Landmarks of Freemasonry is a collection of lectures presented to Craft Lodges over twelve years, following a somewhat daunting task of cataloguing 3,000 Masonic volumes during my six years as Assistant Librarian with the Provincial Grand Lodge of Sussex. None of these had been catalogued since 1947 and it seemed pointless to merely list the title, author and date of publication. What was surely needed was a table of contents, but because so few of them had one, a painstaking investigation often took place, resulting in an 'hourly' advancement in Masonic knowledge.

The process firstly involved sorting out the hundreds of donated volumes, many of which had three, four, five or more copies. They were collected up and then examined for the one in best condition, which was accordingly catalogued onto my laptop. The second best copy was taken home with me and the rest were binned!

Thus a private library of Masonic literature was accumulated. Long after cataloguing all those Masonic volumes, whenever inspired to research the next lecture, such a collection soon provided virtually all the required material; as found in every one of the book's references. The lectures, offered to Lodges as far afield as London and Leeds have so far raised well over £2,500 for various charities. They were all intended to be verbally delivered and have only been sparingly modified for current academic appreciation. The additional collection of lectures also features Royal Arch, Mark and Rose Croix treatises.

CHAPTER ONE

LIVING LANDMARKS OF FREEMASONRY

AS A FREEMASON and also a Freeman of the City of London, I must admit to never having given too much thought to the word *free* in both those personal honours. Perhaps only a few of those reading this paper have either. However, in the course of my research into the landmarks of Freemasonry a surprising truth emerged, which may well cause more than slight consternation. The first question we were all asked at our Initiation was: 'Are you free and of the full age of twenty-one years?'

Some of us may have mentally checked our date of birth when answering 'yes' and also made the assumption that we were free to make up our own minds about joining the Order. None of us could possibly be aware that an important landmark was being observed, which in due course will hopefully become more fully understood. What was really behind the Worshipful Master's question? The truth may well come as a shock;

> Are you free and of the full age of twenty-one years - because I can already ascertain from your naked left breast and your general deportment that you are neither a woman nor a cripple, but what I really need to know is – are you a slave or were you born into slavery!

So let us be clear, the landmarks of interest to us today are not those historical moments in Freemasonry, such as the formation of the United Grand Lodge of England in 1717, the unification of the Ancients and Moderns in 1813 or indeed the introduction from America in 1845 of the *Ancient and Accepted Rite* by Doctor Robert Crucefix, who also in that same year happened to be the Consecrating Officer of my mother Lodge, Zetland Lodge, No. 511.

No, the landmarks of particular interest at the moment have evolved from those physical indicators, which generally help us to find our way around, in the way that the far distant cathedral spire proved such a welcome sight to the traveller long ago, or even the reassuring beams from lighthouses which are visible to the sea captain near to land at night. However, in Biblical times, the Book of Deuteronomy describes them as; 'Enactments and penalties respecting boundaries of estates indicated by certain objects, such as stone pillars which carried a curse on anyone who unlawfully removed their neighbour's landmarks.' Such landmarks could only be altered or removed by mutual agreement, as in the sale by one to another, just as in the establishment of property boundaries today.

The Jewish law in Deuteronomy also states: 'Thou shalt not remove thy neighbour's landmark, which they of old time have set in thine inheritance.' The Hebrew origin of the word *landmark* is apparently *g'vul*, meaning *border,* or *coast* or *line,* which is derived from *gabal,* meaning a rope and suggests that it originally referred to a boundary-line determined by stretching a rope or drawing a straight line connecting point to point, just as with the builder's skirret; 'An implement which acts on a centre pin, whence a line is drawn to mark out the ground for the foundation of the intended structure.'

Ironically, the same word *gabal* in Arabic means *mountain,* as in *gabal Tariq* or Gibraltar as we know it today. A more distinctive landmark for mariners would be hard to imagine. According to Albert Mackey in 1861, 'Those peculiar marks of distinction by which we are enabled to designate our inheritance as the sons of light are called the landmarks of the order. He also adds significantly that; 'It is not in the power of any body of men to make innovations in Masonry.'

A hundred years ago, Brother Chetwode Crawley in his paper on 'The Craft and Its Orphans in the Eighteenth Century' commented that:

> The ancient landmarks of Freemasonry, like all other landmarks, material and symbolic, can only preserve their stability when they reach down to sure foundations. When the philosophic student unearths the underlying rock on which our ancient landmarks rest, he finds our sure foundations in the triple dogma of the fatherhood of God, the brotherhood of man, and the life to come. All laws, customs and methods that obtain amongst us, and do not ultimately find footholds on this basis, are thereby earmarked as conventions and conveniences, in no way partaking of the nature of ancient landmarks.

More recently in 1958, Herbert Inman gave the following definitions of a landmark:

a) Leading and essential characteristics.
b) Leading principles from which there can be no deviation.
c) Universal laws of Masonry.
d) Ceremonies, rules and laws deemed absolutely necessary.
e) Immemorial and universal observances.

In fact, our Craft ritual contains many references to landmarks. The Initiate for instance is told that his fidelity: '…must be exemplified by a strict observance of the constitutions of the fraternity and by adhering to the ancient landmarks of the Order.'

The Fellow Craft, is again referred to them in the course of his passing, and urged that the former charge neither is nor ever would be effaced from his memory. In the *Charge after Raising,* the Master Mason is reminded that: '…the ancient landmarks of the order, which are entrusted to your care, you are to preserve sacred and inviolable.' During his obligation, the Master Elect solemnly promises that he will not: '…either during his Mastership or at any time the Lodge may be under his direction, permit or suffer any deviation from the ancient customs and established landmarks of the Order.'

Now we must take account of the various mentions of the subject in our *Book of Constitutions*; The 1738 *Constitutions* repeat the earlier 1723 statement, when they declare that the Grand Lodge possesses the supreme superintending authority and alone has the power of enacting laws and regulations for the governing of the Craft, and of altering, repealing, and abrogating them, '...always taking care that the ancient landmarks of the Order are preserved.'

Regulation 55 stipulates that should the Grand Master consider that any proposed resolution at the Quarterly Communications of Grand Lodge contain anything contrary to the ancient landmarks, he may refuse to permit it to be discussed. This particular authority descends through the body of Freemasonry to the Master Elect, who is required to confirm that, '...it is not within the power of any man or body of men to make innovation in the body of Masonry.' On the subject of innovation, Bernard Jones in 1950 added this pertinent observation:

> To the customs, practices, tenets, traditions and observances that can be proved to have existed from time immemorial, some Brethren would add any customs, even if not ancient, that are universally acknowledged. But, against this, it is solidly contended that were it possible for the Freemasons of the whole world to come together and agree on a new and common belief they would not and could not by so doing create a landmark!

It is held that a landmark can be discovered, but not created; it cannot be changed or obliterated. Thus a world concourse of Masons, unable to create a landmark, would in conclusion be equally unable to obliterate one. The landmarks of the Order, like the laws of the Medes and the Persians, can suffer no change, 'What they were centuries ago, they still remain, and must so continue until Freemasonry itself shall cease to exist.'

Now we come to the crucial question, at regular intervals throughout his Masonic progression, a Freemason is charged with a duty of observing and preserving the ancient landmarks and established customs of the Order. It may therefore come as a surprise to learn that even the United Grand Lodge of England, while on the one hand stipulating that they must be always be observed and never changed, in their infinite wisdom have actually declined to define or specify any of them. Furthermore, we hear of the *landmarks being in danger* when any attempt is made, for example, to correct a misquotation or a grammatical error in the ritual, and there is also the general practice of grouping all customs, usages and landmarks together; and assuming that they are all one and the same thing, which cannot be true.

In trying to determine the exact definitions of the Landmarks of Freemasonry, there has been plenty of disagreement and diversity of opinion among writers. Some simply restrict them to the signs, tokens, and words during meetings. Some include the ceremonies of initiation, passing, and raising, while others prefer to class as landmarks the form, dimensions and support, or perhaps the ornaments, furniture, and jewels of a Lodge. Some believe that the Order has no landmarks at all except perhaps its peculiar secrets. But all of these are woolly and unconvincing definitions – excluding those that are obvious, and admitting others that are less so.

Perhaps the safest method is to restrict them to those ancient, and therefore universal, customs of the Order, which either gradually grew into operation as rules of conduct, or, if once adopted by any competent authority, were created so long ago, that no account of their origin is to be found in the records of history. Both the creators and any record of their creation have long passed away, and the landmarks are therefore, '…of higher antiquity than memory or history can reach.' The first requisite, therefore, of a custom or rule of conduct to constitute it a landmark, is that it must have existed from time immemorial; its antiquity is its essential element.

So how many landmarks in fact are there? Well, one of the most prolific Masonic authors of all time was the Reverend George Oliver, who in 1832 was Provincial Deputy Grand Master of Lincolnshire. Apart from writing a *History of Freemasonry from 1829 to 1841* and the two volume *Historical Landmarks of Freemasonry*, he lists in his *Treasury of Freemasonry,* as many as forty landmarks, together with another twelve, which were either spurious or obsolete. However, Albert Mackey is generally credited with narrowing them down to twenty five in his 1858 *Encyclopaedia of Freemasonry*.

Broadly speaking they fall into five categories: but his primary landmark is a belief in one Supreme Being and acceptance of the indispensable rule that the Volume of the Sacred Law should be displayed open while every Lodge is at labour. The five general categories are:

The equality of all Freemasons
Secrecy of modes of recognition
The modes themselves
That every Lodge shall be tyled
The government of a Lodge by the Master and his Wardens

Strangely, although the opening of the Volume of the Sacred Law at every Masonic meeting is generally viewed as the Brotherhood's principle landmark, it fails to achieve recognition until number twenty one of Mackey's universally accepted list of twenty five landmarks, which begins with the manner in which two strangers can instantly identify each other as Freemasons.

The modes of recognition are, of all the landmarks, the most legitimate and unquestioned. They admit of no variation; and, if ever they have suffered alteration or addition, the evil of such a violation of the ancient law has always made itself subsequently manifest. The next two landmarks define the place of the three degrees in our ceremonies and the mystical importance of the Hiramic Legend as central to our Masonic identity.

The division of Symbolic Freemasonry into three Degrees is a landmark that has been better preserved than almost any other. In 1813, the Grand Lodge of England vindicated the Ancient Landmark, by solemnly enacting that Ancient Craft Masonry consisted of the three Degrees of Entered Apprentice, Fellow-Craft, and Master Mason, including the Holy Royal Arch. But, the disruption has never been healed, and the landmark, although acknowledged in its integrity by all still continues to be violated.

The Legend of the Third Degree is an important landmark, the integrity of which has been well preserved. There is no Rite of Freemasonry, practiced in any country or language, in which the essential elements of this Legend are not taught. The Lectures may vary, and indeed are constantly changing, but the Legend has ever remained substantially the same, and it is necessary that it should be so, for the legend of the Temple Builder constitutes the very essence and identity of Freemasonry. Any Rite, which should exclude it, or materially alter it, would at once, by that exclusion or alteration, cease to be a Masonic Rite.

We now move on to the upper echelons of the Fraternity, in particular the need to appoint a Grand Master to oversee our activities, as clearly defined in the next five landmarks. The government of the Fraternity by a presiding officer called a Grand Master, who is elected from the body of the Craft, is a fourth landmark of the Order. There are many who suppose that the election of the Grand Master is held in consequence of a law or regulation of the Grand Lodge. Such, however, is not the case. Grand Masters, or persons performing the functions under a different but equivalent title, are to be found in the records of the Institution long before Grand Lodges were established; and if the present system of legislative government by Grand Lodges were to be abolished, a Grand Master would still be necessary.

The prerogative of the Grand Master to preside over every Assembly of the Craft, wherever and whenever held, is a fifth landmark. It is in consequence of this law, derived from ancient usage, and not from any special enactment, that the Grand Master assumes the chair, or as it is called in England, the throne, at every Communication of the Grand Lodge; and that he is also entitled to preside at the communication of every subordinate Lodge, where he may happen to be present.

The Grand Master' prerogative to grant Dispensations for conferring Degrees at irregular times is another important landmark. The statutory law of Freemasonry requires a month, or other determinate period, to elapse between the presentation of a petition and the election of a candidate. But the Grand Master has the power to set aside or dispense with this probation, and to allow a candidate to be initiated at once. The prerogative of the Grand Master to give Dispensations for opening and holding Lodges is another landmark. He may grant in virtue of this, to a sufficient number of Freemasons, the privilege of meeting together and conferring Degrees. The Lodges thus established are called Lodges under Dispensation.

The privilege of the Grand Master to make Freemasons at sight is a landmark, which is closely connected with the preceding one. The Emperor of Germany and the

Duke of Newcastle were made Freemasons in this way in 1731. There were a few other instances, but the perhaps the most significant was in 1787, when the Prince of Wales was initiated at the Star and Garter Tavern, Pall Mall (When the Duke of Cumberland and the Grand Master, presided in person.) We now discover the importance of our Lodge meetings, which are clearly defined, right down to the composition of its Officers, including the Tyler, whose situation is vital, whenever the Lodge is at labour.

The necessity for Freemasons to congregate in Lodges is another landmark. It is not to be understood by this that any ancient landmark has directed that permanent organisation of subordinate Lodges which constitutes one of the features of the Masonic system as it now prevails. But, the landmarks of the Order always prescribed that Freemasons should, from time to time, congregate together for the purpose of either Operative or Speculative labour, and that these Congregations should be called Lodges.

The government of the Craft, when so congregated in a Lodge by a Master and two Wardens, is also a landmark. A congregation of Freemasons meeting together under any other government, as that, for instance, of a president and vice-president, or a chairman and sub-chairman, would not be recognised as a Lodge. The presence of a Master and two Wardens is as essential to the valid organisation of a Lodge as a Warrant of Constitution is at the present day. The names, of course, vary in different languages; but the officers, their number, prerogatives, and duties are everywhere identical.

The necessity that every Lodge, when congregated, should be duly Tyled is an important landmark of the Institution, which is never neglected. The necessity of this law arises from the esoteric character of Freemasonry. The duty of guarding the door, and keeping off cowans and eavesdroppers is an ancient one, which therefore constitutes a landmark.

The following landmarks address the rights of individual Brethren, in particular the right of free association and the need to be represented. Also mentioned is the need to prove the Masonic credentials of all visitors, '…less by neglect the members present should be innocently led to violate their obligation.' Similarly, the right of every Freemason to be represented in all general meetings of the Craft, and to instruct his representatives, is a twelfth landmark. Formerly, these general meetings, which were usually held once a year, were called General Assemblies, and all the Fraternity, even to the youngest Entered Apprentice, was permitted to be present. Now they are called Grand Lodges, and only the Masters and Wardens of the subordinate Lodges are summoned. But this is simply as the representatives of their members. Originally, each Freemason represented himself; now he is represented by his officers.

The right of every Freemason to appeal from the decision of his Brethren, in Lodge convened, to the Grand Lodge or General Assembly of Freemasons, is a landmark highly essential to the preservation of justice, and the prevention of oppression. The right of every Freemason to visit and sit in every regular Lodge is an unquestionable landmark of the Order. This is called the right of visitation. This right of visitation has always been recognised as an inherent right, which insures to every Freemason as he travels through the world, and this is because Lodges are justly considered as only divisions for convenience of the universal Masonic family.

Furthermore, it is a landmark of the Order, that no visitor unknown to the Brethren present, or to some one of them as a Freemason, can enter a Lodge without first passing an examination according to ancient usage. Of course, if the visitor is known to any Brother present to be a Freemason in good standing, and if that Brother will vouch for his qualifications, the examination may be dispensed with, as the landmark refers only to the cases of strangers, '…who are not to be recognised unless after strict trial, due examination, or lawful information.'

What the Lodge may do is one thing, but the remaining landmarks clearly define the restrictions on Lodge activities with respect to its effect on other Lodges. The first of which clearly defines exactly who can and cannot be admitted as a member of our Noble Fraternity; then the paramount qualification of every candidate, to acknowledge the existence of a Supreme Being, and finally the necessity for the Volume of the Sacred Law to form the centre piece of any Lodge meeting. But now we must encounter the shock revelation made at the opening of this very lecture.

Certain qualifications of candidates for initiation are derived from a landmark of the order. These qualifications are that he shall be a man, un-mutilated, free born, and of mature age.

That is to say, '… a woman, a cripple, or a slave, or one born into slavery is disqualified for initiation into the Rites of Freemasonry.' Statutes have from time to time been enacted, enforcing or explaining this principle; but the qualifications really arise from the very nature of the Masonic Institution and from its symbolic teachings. It is worth reminding ourselves that the only reference on which more than two centuries of argument has been based, was when Dr Anderson used the word *landmark* in Rule 39 of his 1723 *Book of Constitution*s. He was of course merely using a portmanteau word, as was his custom, without intending to attach to it any precise meaning whatsoever. It is worth repeating that all Dr Anderson actually wrote was that the Regulations could be added to or altered by Grand Lodge, 'Provided always that the old landmarks be carefully preserved.'

However, the modern view, with which there is likely to be general, but of course not universal agreement, is along the lines of an American Mason's opinion, that a landmark is that without which Freemasonry cannot exist and which determines the boundary beyond which Grand Lodge cannot step. Anything in Freemasonry that a Grand Lodge is empowered to change cannot possibly be a landmark. Indeed the final Landmark spells this out clearly. The last and crowning landmark of all is that these landmarks can never be changed. Nothing can be subtracted from them, nothing can be added to them, not the slightest modification can be made in them. As they were received from our predecessors, we are bound by the most solemn obligations of duty to transmit them to our successors.

Ultimately, Bernard Jones concludes that all freethinking Freemasons will want to make their own search for what they regard as the landmarks, and that what one Brother finds, may not exactly agree with what another may discover. The real question is, would Freemasonry mean as much to him if its landmarks were altered or removed? If the answer is 'yes', then he will have to continue his search, but successful or not, we trust he will find that the very act of looking for an answer, brings its own reward.

References:

Dr J. Anderson, *Constitutions*, 1723 & 1738 - Bernard Quaritch Ltd London, 1923

Albert Mackey, *Encyclopaedia of Freemasonry*, Griffin, Bohn & Co, London 1875

Kenneth Mackenzie, *Royal Masonic Cyclopaedia*, John Hogg, London 1877

Chetwode Crawley, 'Ars Quatuor Coronati', Quatuor Coronati , London 1889

Arthur Waite, *New Encyclopaedia of Freemasonry*, Rider & Co. London 1918

B. Jones, *Freemason's Guide and Compendium*, George Harrap, London 1950

Herbert Inman, *Masonic Problems and Queries*, A. Lewis, London 1957

CHAPTER TWO

1723 AND ALL THAT

Constitutions *(Anderson's Constitutions c.1723)*

A FACSIMILE COPY of the 1723 *Book of Constitutions* came recently into my warm and appreciative hands. Surprisingly, it not only included a fifty-two page introduction by Lionel Vibert, a Past Master of Quatuor Coronati Lodge, but also an opening forty-eight page history of the Craft by Dr James Anderson, before we eventually come across, *The Charges of a Freemason, extracted from the Ancient Records of Lodges beyond the Sea, and those of England, Scotland and Ireland, for the use of Lodges in London.*

As a Freemason, I am a firm believer in a Divine Being, and I am also aware that some Freemasons, who follow Creationist doctrines, accept the Book of Genesis as a reasonable explanation for our earthly existence. What I do find difficult to acknowledge, as an evolutionist, is that Freemasons of the early eighteenth century were required not only to abide by the rules and regulations printed in 1723, but also to accept a genealogy of Freemasonry, apparently dating right back to the time of Adam and Eve.

> Once established on this earth and introduced to the seductive charms of Eve, Adam apparently developed the theoretical skills, much later identified and perfected by Euclid: As Dr Anderson claims: No doubt Adam taught his sons Geometry, and the use of it, in the several Arts and Crafts convenient, at least, for those early times; for Cain we find built a City, which he called after the name of his eldest Son, Enoch; and becoming the Prince of one half of mankind, his posterity would imitate his Royal example in improving both the noble Science and the useful art, as other arts were also improved by them, for instance working in metal by Tubal Cain, music by Jubal, pasturage and tent-making by Jabal, which last is good architecture.

Now, we are further informed that:

> ...without regarding uncertain accounts, we may safely conclude the old world, that lasted 1,656 years, could not be ignorant of Masonry; and that both the families of Seth and Cain erected many curious works until at length Noah, the ninth from Seth, was commanded and directed by God to build a great Ark, which though of wood, was certainly fabricated by Geometry, and according to the rules of Masonry.

It is not long before Freemasonry is identified in Egypt:

> ...because we find the River Nile's overflowing its banks, soon caused an improvement in Geometry, which consequently brought Masonry much in request: For the ancient noble cities, with the other magnificent edifices of that country, and particularly the famous Pyramids, demonstrate the early taste and genius of that ancient Kingdom. Indeed, one of those Egyptian Pyramids is reckoned the first of the Seven Wonders of the World.

Perhaps it is no coincidence that the arrival of *Sojourners* soon offers our Royal Arch Degree the relevance it seeks:

> The select family long used military architecture only, as they were Sojourners among strangers; but before year 430, so their peregrinations were expire. Even about 86 years before the Exodus, the Kings of Egypt forced most of them to lay down their shepherd's instruments, and warlike accoutrements, and trained them to another sort of architecture in stone and brick, as Holy writ, and other histories acquaint us; which God did wisely over-rule, in order to make them good Masons before they possessed the promised land, then famous for most curious Masonry.

The *Book of Constitutions* then introduces us to the building of King Solomon's Temple, but not before mentioning the earlier Temple of Dagon in Gaza, which we are reminded was capacious enough to receive 5000 people under its roof and which was cleverly supported by two main columns. These were eventually pulled down by Samson, bringing about the Temple's destruction. Anderson explains that his association with Delilah prevented him from being awarded the honour to be numbered among Masons. He then writes, '…but it is not convenient to write more of this!'

It was Solomon's great Temple at Jerusalem:

> …begun and finished, to the amazement of the world, in the short space of seven years and six months, by that wisest of man and most glorious King of Israel, the Prince of Peace and Architecture, Solomon (the Son of David, who was refused the honour for being a man of blood) by Divine direction, without the noise of workmen's tools, though there were employed about it no less than 3,600 Princes or Master Masons, to conduct the work according to Solomon's directions, with 80,000 hewers of stone in the mountain, or Fellow Craftsmen, and 70,000 labourers, in all 153,600 besides the levy under Adoniram to work in the mountains of Lebanon, by turns with the Sidonians.

That's 153,600 workers needing to be fed each day. So let's say one cook for every twenty workers: 7,680 cooks, who themselves also need to eat; 161,280 meals a day for seven and a half years comes to a staggering 44 million platefuls for the festive board! Something has surely been greatly exaggerated. Exactly where and how food supplies were sourced remains a mystery, given the passage of the seasons from summer to winter, not to mention the immense transport logistics to be overcome, and don't even think about toilets! Bearing in mind, the kind of workforce needed to construct Saint Paul's Cathedral, for example, we can only deduce that the numbers were vastly exaggerated. Indeed there are no contemporary records to support such grandiose claims.

We next read that:

Solomon was much obliged to the King of Tyre, who sent his masons and carpenters to Jerusalem, and the firs and cedars of Lebanon to Joppa the next sea-port. But above all, he sent his namesake Hiram or Huram, the most accomplished Mason upon Earth.

Here the footnotes become convoluted, in the author's attempt to identify Hiram Abif from the biblical quote from 1 Kings v. 14:

…and King Solomon sent and fetched Hiram out of Tyre. He was a widow's son of the tribe of Naphtali, and his father was a man of Tyre, a worker in brass; and he was filled with wisdom, and understanding and cunning to work all work in brass. And he came to King Solomon, and wrought all his work, for he cast two pillars of brass, of eighteen cubits high apiece; and a line of twelve cubits did compass either of them about.

The subsequent thirty verses detail the intricate skills of Hiram in elaborate metalwork, even down to making brass pots, shovels and basins. Of course the two pillars were set up in the porch of the Temple, '…and he set up the right pillar, and called the name thereof Jachin; and he set up the left pillar, and called the name thereof Boaz.' Sadly, Hiram's architectural prowess is hardly mentioned, although in 2 Chronicles Chapter Two, we read of this message from Hiram King of Tyre:

…and now I have sent a cunning man, endued with understanding, of Huram my fathers, The son of a woman of Dan, and his father was a man of Tyre, skilful to work in gold and in silver, in brass, in iron, in stone and in timber, in purple, in blue and in fine linen and in crimson; also to grave any manner of graving, and to find out every device which shall be put to him, with thy cunning men, and with the cunning men of my lord David thy father.

Despite all his previously mentioned skills it was King Solomon, who by all accounts took responsibility for the actual Temple construction.

2 Chronicles, Chapter Three begins thus:

Then Solomon began to build the house of the Lord at Jerusalem in Mount Moriah, where the Lord appeared unto David, his father, in the place that David had prepared in the threshing floor of Ornan the Jebusite. And he began to build in the second month, in the fourth year of his reign.

The Chapter continues with a detailed account of the dimensions and construction of the temple, then finally attributes just the brass work to Huram:

> ...and Huram made the pots and the shovels, and the basins, and Huram finished the work that he was to make for King Solomon for the house of God: to wit, the two pillars and the pommels, and the chapiters which were on top of the two pillars, and the two wreathes to cover the two pommels of the chapiters which were on the top of the pillars.

It would appear from the above that Hiram was only ever going to be identified in Chapter Four with all the brass work, while credit for the actual stone construction was going to be assumed solely by King Solomon. Thus in the *Book of Constitutions*, Anderson regales us with his personal vision of King Solomon's Masonic achievements:

> This most sumptuous, splendid, beautiful, and glorious edifice, attracted soon the inquisitive artists of all nations to spend some time at Jerusalem and survey its peculiar Excellencies, as much as was allowed to the gentiles; whereby they soon discovered that all the world, with their joint skill, came far short of the Israelites, in the wisdom and dexterity of architecture, when the wise King Solomon was Grand Master of the Lodge at Jerusalem, and the learned King Hiram was Grand Master of the Lodge at Tyre, and the inspired Hiram Abif was under the immediate care and direction of Heaven, when the noble and wise thought it their honour to be assisting the ingenious Masters and Craftsmen, and when the temple of the true God became the wonder of all travellers, by which, they corrected the Architecture of their own country upon their return.

We now turn to English history and Anderson's claim that:

> ...though the ancient records of the Brotherhood in England were many of them destroyed or lost in the wars of the Saxons and Danes, yet King Athelstan, a mighty architect, the first anointed King of England, and who translated the Holy Bible into the Saxon tongue, when he had brought the land into rest and peace, built many great works and encouraged many Masons from France, who were appointed Overseers thereof, and brought with them the Charges and Regulations of the Lodges preserved from Roman times, who also prevailed with the King to improve the constitution of the English Lodges, according to the foreign model and to increase the wages of working Masons.

There appears to be no current evidence that Athelstan actually translated the Bible into Saxon, although Anderson appears to be quoting the *Regius* manuscript of 1390:

This craft came into England, as I tell you, in the time of good King Athelstan's reign; he made then both hall, and also bower and lofty temples of great honor, to take his recreation in both day and night and to worship his God with all his might. This good Lord loved this craft full well, and purposed to strengthen it in every part on account of various defects that he discovered in the craft. He sent about into all the land, after all the Masons of the craft, to come straight to him, to amend all these defects by good counsel, if it might so happen.

According to Albert Mackey, a *Book of Constitutions* published by J. Roberts the previous year includes the following:

Athelstan began to build many Abbeys, Monasteries and other religious houses, as also Castles and diverse fortresses for defence of his realm. He loved Masons more than his father; he greatly studied Geometry, and sent into many lands for men expert in the science. He gave them a very large charter to hold a yearly assembly, and power to correct offenders in the said science; and the King himself caused a general assembly of all Masons in his realm, at York, and there were made many Masons, and gave them a deep charge for observation of all such articles as belonged unto Masonry and delivered them into the said Charter to keep.

The year was actually 926, and Athelstan had only just ascended the throne and was busy pursuing the sons of the recently deceased King of Northumbria, whom he had vowed to dethrone. Mackey argues it was unlikely:

…that while pursuing the sons of Stigtryg, one of whom had escaped his captors and taken refuge in the city of York, whose citizens he vainly sought to enlist in his favour, Athelstan would have selected that period of conflict and a city within his newly-acquired territory, instead of his own Capital, for the time and place of holding an assembly of Masons.

By 1722 George Payne, a Grand Master, had prepared an acceptable version of that part of the Old Charges (the important half) which was called the Old Regulations. By the following year, Grand Lodge, reporting through a Committee headed by James Anderson, adopted a completed manuscript, entitled *The Constitution of Freemasons*, and had James Anderson print it.

Albert Mackey wonders why this book was accredited to the authorship of James Anderson; he is called author at one or two places but at that time the word could mean editor or compiler; and his name does not appear on the title page. George Payne wrote about fifty per cent of it. John Theophilus Desaguliers wrote the dedication; the rest of it was the joint work of many hands and at least two Committees. The so-called historical part was assembled, the record in fact says collated from Lodge copies of the Old Charges, which differed very much among themselves in detail.

It is commonly accepted that Freemasonry as we know it today, evolved from Operative Masonry. It is also without doubt that any ruler, from King Solomon onwards, who wished to be remembered for all time, would seek to leave a substantial architectural edifice as a monument to his status. What greater legacy for example is there than the pyramids of Egypt? Every stone would need to be precisely shaped, and hundreds of workmen would be required to bring the rude matter into due form. The skilled workmen fashioning ashlars for any architectural project would certainly expect to be paid and would employ apprentices to ease the workload.

Just like any tradesmen, a guild of operatives would negotiate appropriate food and accommodation for the duration. However, just as trade unions today decide policy and procedure, without any signs or symbols other than a warm handshake being exchanged, it is pure conjecture on behalf of those seeking to manufacture a link between the development of Egyptian, Roman, Greek or Anglo-Saxon stonemasons and the current rituals of speculative Freemasonry.

The old manuscripts were generally inaccessible to the Fraternity and indeed, until comparatively recently, few of them have been discovered. It is thanks to the publication of the legend by Anderson, and subsequently by Preston, that we are able to attribute its general adoption by the Craft for more than a couple of centuries.

The origin of English Freemasonry at York in 926 is sometimes called the York Legend and sometimes the Athelstan Legend. This is because the General Assembly, said to have been held there, occurred during the reign of that King. However, the form of the legend, as given by Anderson in his first edition, varies slightly from that in his second. In the former, he places the date of the York Ritual at 930; in his second, at 926. Also in the first he styles the congregation at York a General Lodge, but in his second, he calls it a Grand Lodge. As the modern and universally accepted form of the legend agrees in both respects with the latter statement, and not with the earlier version, we must conclude that the second edition has become the currently adopted and popular form.

Such is the York Legend, as it has been accepted by the Craft, contained in all the old manuscripts from at least the end of the fourteenth century to the present day; officially sanctioned by Anderson, the historian of the Grand Lodge in 1723, and repeated by Preston, by Oliver, and by almost all succeeding Masonic writers. Only recently has anyone thought of doubting its authenticity; and now the important question in Masonic literature is whether it is in fact a myth or a history, whether it is all or in any part fiction or truth, and if so, what proportion belongs to the former and what to the latter category. In reaching a conclusion on this subject, the question necessarily divides itself into three forms:

1. Was there an Assembly of Freemasons held in or about the year 926, at York, under the patronage or by the permission of King Athelstan? There is actually nothing in the personal character or the political conduct of

Athelstan that rules out such a possibility or even probability. He was liberal in his ideals, like his grandfather the great Alfred; he was a promoter of civilisation; he patronised learning, built many churches and monasteries, encouraged the translation of the Scriptures, and gave charters too many operative companies.

2. Was Edwin, the brother of Athelstan, the person who convoked that Assembly? This question has frequently been discussed with the suggestion that the Edwin alluded to in the legend was not the son or brother of Athelstan, but Edwin, King of Northumbria. Doctor Mackey believes that Francis Drake, in his speech before the Grand Lodge of York in 1726 was the first to publicly advance this opinion; but he does so in a way that shows that the view must have been generally accepted by his auditors. He says:

> …you know we can boast that the first Grand Lodge ever held in England was held in this city, where Edwin, the first Christian King of Northumbria, about the six hundredth year after Christ, and who laid the foundation of our Cathedral, sat as Grand Master.

Edwin, who was born in 586, ascended the throne in 617, and died in 633. He was pre-eminent, among the Anglo-Saxon Kings for his military genius and statesmanship. The chief event of his reign was the introduction of Christianity throughout his Kingdom.

Previous to Edwin's reign, the northern metropolis of the Church had been placed at York. The only objection to this theory is its date, which is three hundred years before the reign of Athelstan and the supposed assembly at York in 926.

3. Are the Constitutions, which were adopted by that General Assembly now in existence? It is not to be doubted, that if a General Assembly was held, it must have adopted Constitutions or regulations for the government of the Craft. That would be the main object of such a meeting. But there is insufficient evidence that the Regulations now called the York Constitutions or the Gothic Constitutions are those that were adopted in 926.

It is more probable that the original document and all genuine copies of it are lost, and that it formed the prototype from which all the more modern manuscript Constitutions have been formed. There is the strongest evidence that all the manuscripts, from the Halliwell to the Papworth, have a common origin, from which they were copied with more or less accuracy, or on which they were framed with more or less modification.

Doctor Mackey supposed this original to be the very Constitutions, which were adopted at the General Assembly at York. His conclusions may safely be advanced on this subject, until there are better reasons than we now have to reject them. That is, somewhere around the year 926 a General Assembly of Operative Freemasons was held at York, under the patronage of Edwin, brother of Athelstan, at which a code of laws was adopted, which became the basis on which all subsequent Masonic Constitutions appear to have been framed.

The absence of any original documentary evidence brings us full circle to my opening comments about fellow Freemasons who follow Creationist doctrines, in denial of the carbon dating of prehistoric evidence. Sadly both Neanderthal and Cro-Magnon remains indicate the kind of ancestors, which boldly deny the existence of Adam and Eve. Indeed, skeletons of the latter were discovered in the Cro-Magnon cave at Dordogne in France. The remains were those of three adult males, one adult female, and one infant.

Our immediate ancestors lived from about 45,000 to 10,000 years ago in the Upper Palaeolithic period of the Pleistocene epoch. They apparently co-existed with Neanderthal man for a time, but eventually drove them into extinction. They were tall — just like modern humans — their skull had no brow ridges, and was rounded with a high forehead and with a projecting chin. The Cro-Magnon brain size was the same as today, about 1,350 millilitres. As their oral anatomy was identical to modern humans, it is most likely that they could probably speak. Sadly the word 'Geometry' was unlikely to have been in their everyday vocabulary.

It logically follows that the exception proves the rule, and where Dr Anderson and his fellow writers could reasonably have expected the Masonic rank and file to accept without question a hypothetical evolution of the Craft based on Bible history, today's more widely informed readers may generally take his fanciful claims with a pinch of salt. Although like the symbolic nature of our ritual, if it helps us to make sense of our existence either as Christians or Freemasons, then … so mote it be.

References:

Dr J. Anderson, *Constitutions*, 1723, 1738 & 1756 - Bernard Quaritch Ltd, London, 1923

Albert Mackey, *Encyclopaedia of Freemasonry*, Griffin, Bohn & Co, London 1873/78

R.F. Gould, *History of Freemasonry*, Thomas Jack, London 1886

E. Waite, *New Encyclopaedia of Freemasonry*, Rider & Co. London 1918

CHAPTER THREE

FATHER CHRISTMAS AND CHARITABLE GIVING

WHEN THE ROLL-ON roll-off ferry, Herald of Free Enterprise capsized shortly after leaving Zeebrugge on March 6th 1987, one of the 188 victims was Worshipful Brother Brian Eades, who had just been installed as the Master of Corinthian Lodge No. 1208 in Dover, and had not yet performed a ceremony. The Province of East Kent subsequently planted a field with 188 trees in honour of the victims to be known as Herald Wood.

On July 17th, 1998, a tsunami in Papua New Guinea killed 2,200. Once again, Kent Freemasons were not slow to react. The Provincial Grand Master, John Bonomy, immediately contributed £10,000 and then wrote to each of his Lodges informing them that the Provincial coffers were now bare, and inviting them to send replacement funds as soon as possible, on the basis that when victims need financial assistance, they need it straight away, not after committees have been formed and several weeks have passed.

Until the National Lottery was established, Freemasonry was the largest single charitable organisation in the United Kingdom. Millions are still raised each year with hardly any publicity. What is not usually appreciated by the public is that whereas other creditable organisations such as Lions and Rotary raise large amounts for worthwhile causes, this is achieved by shaking tins in the High Street, whereas a Freemason's giving is always straight from the pocket.

So what are the origins of charitable giving among Freemasons? Just as our working tools owe their existence to those of operative stonemasons, so also have we inherited their practice of nurturing those less fortunate than themselves. The old operative fraternities were not indifferent to the needs of their distressed members. Their *Manuscript Charges* advocated receiving and cherishing foreign operatives by offering them work or helping them on their journeys. Medieval operative Lodges in Scotland appear to have been efficient in this respect. Members' dues were placed in a box which was looked after by the box master or treasurer, specifically for the assistance of distressed Brethren and for the education of the orphans of deceased members. Fines levied against members who were rude or intemperate at meetings were also placed in the box.

By contrast the development of *Speculative* Lodges did not place charitable giving as high on the agenda. There may be a very simple explanation. Its members, not originating from the working classes in the seventeenth century, were far less likely to be in need of financial assistance. Any Brother who fell into difficulties would probably be offered funds by his more wealthy companions. With the formation of the first Grand Lodge of England in 1717, charitable giving began to be promoted for the benefit of those poorer members of society whose numbers were beginning to swell its ranks.

It was Dr James Anderson's first *Book of Constitutions* in 1723, which laid down a version of the operative *Manuscript Charges*. These originally outlined a stonemason's duties, not only to God and his master, but also to his family and those around him. They specifically mentioned fellow masons seeking work thus: '...if you discover him to be a true and genuine Brother, you are to respect him accordingly; and if he is in want, you must relieve him if you can, or else direct him to how he might be relieved.'

Today, the newly initiated Entered Apprentice standing at the North East corner, poor and penniless, is encouraged to acknowledge and understand his charitable obligations. Back In 1861, Albert Mackey defined Masonic Charity:

> Charity is the cornerstone of our temple and, upon it is to be erected a superstructure of all the other virtues, which make the good man and the good Mason. The charity, however, of which our order boasts, is not alone that sentiment of commiseration, which leads us to assist the poor with pecuniary donations. Like the virtue described by the apostle, its application is more and more extensive. It suffereth long and is kind.

Of course, the three grand principles on which Freemasonry is founded are brotherly love, relief and truth, the second of which is generally believed to be charity, but only 60 years ago the Emulation lectures preferred this interpretation:

> To relieve the distressed is a duty incumbent on all men, particularly Masons, who are linked together in one indissoluble chain of sincere affection; hence to soothe the unhappy, sympathise in their misfortunes, compassionate their miseries and restore peace to their troubled minds, is the grand aim we have in view; on this basis we establish our friendships and form our connections.

The first *Book of Constitutions* in 1723 made clear however that Lodges should choose the most prudent and effective method of collecting and dispersing monies accrued for charitable purposes. However, Grand Lodge soon decided that while it was appropriate for Lodges to assist impoverished Masons on an individual basis, it might be more efficient to establish a central Charity Fund.

In 1727, a Charity Committee was established, and was empowered to consider petitions and to grant assistance of up to five guineas in each case. Lodges were invited to make voluntary contributions and a Grand Treasurer was appointed to manage a charity account, with appropriate oversight by Grand Lodge. Throughout the 18th century the Charity fund grew in popularity, but there were sometimes problems caused by overseas Lodges who made their contributions in gold. These would first have to be assayed and they were sometimes revealed to contain impurities. The Treasurer would then list in his accounts the supposed value of the gold on the credit side and on the debit side, a 'short gold' entry indicating the difference between the supposed and actual value of the contribution. Another problem was caused by fraudsters obtaining funds from Almoners of different Lodges.

In 1902, W.Bro. William Pownall published a pamphlet giving: '…the list of names of Masonic imposters and the undeserving persons who make a practice of habitually seeking assistance from the Almoner's funds in different parts of the country.' Having used various aliases including David Hanson, George Green and Arthur Cutler, a culprit was detected at Ashton-under-Lyme on Sept 3rd 1897, by the Almoner, Brother J. Morton, after having obtained relief on three previous occasions in the name of E. Bennet, J. Philips and H. Dawson. On April 18th 1898, James Hadfield was given 3 months hard labour at Huddersfield for obtaining relief by false pretences.

Much earlier, in 1751 a rival Grand Lodge was established by the *Antients* who immediately formed a Stewards Lodge to manage their Charity funds, but decided to ensure a regular charitable income by instigating compulsory dues, rather than depending on the variable generosity of its Lodges. They amounted to half-a-crown (12½ pence) each quarter, in addition to registration fees for new members.

In 1813, following the union of the two Grand Lodges a Lodge of Benevolence was formed, managed by a Committee of all present and past Grand Officers and the Masters of all Lodges. Its remit was to handle petitions and to grant up to £10 to a distressed Brother or £5 each to widows and orphans. In exceptional cases the Grand Master could authorise payments of up to £20 per petitioner. Sadly, the monthly attendance was very irregular and in 1850 the rules were altered to limit the committee to twelve nominated Past Masters, and after 1870 the Grand Master also created a Board of Benevolence. Its more recent function was to channel the Craft's donations to other Masonic Charities, including the Royal Masonic Institution for Girls and also for Boys and the Royal Masonic Benevolent Institution.

It was through the Board of Benevolence that for over two centuries the Craft has given discreetly and generously to many non-Masonic Charities, as well as supporting numerous appeals in times of local emergency or as a result of national or international disasters. Generally speaking, the degrees beyond the Craft and Royal Arch do not have their own separate charities, but they do have benevolent funds, from which to dispense help to the poor and needy among their members.

Back in 1759, an Italian by the name of Bartholomew Ruspini arrived in England and as a surgeon dentist soon found himself a Royal client in the mother of King George II. He was initiated into Freemasonry in 1762 and took lodgings opposite his most famous client, the Prince of Wales at Carlton House. As his Masonic career progressed, he developed the idea of creating a school for orphans or impoverished daughters of Freemasons, which was soon supported by the Grand Master, the Duke of Cumberland, who agreed to become its Grand Patron.

In order to qualify for admittance the rules stated that:

…in admission of children, preference be given to orphans whose fathers at the time of their decease were registered Freemasons and members of a Lodge. After these a preference to be given to such children whose fathers are members of a Lodge at the time of presenting their petition, but none be admitted but children of registered Masons.

The Royal Masonic Institution for Girls as it quickly became known, soon outgrew its original premises near London's Euston Station and in 1795 it was moved to purpose built premises in Westminster Bridge Road. By 1852 this too became outgrown and a larger building was constructed on Wandsworth common, which was formally opened by the Grand Master, the Earl of Zetland. The Institution aimed to provide a rudimentary education, enabling orphans or girls from impoverished families to obtain work as domestic servants.

There were 33 house rules, the final rule being, 'Every well-behaved girl on leaving shall have, Gowns, Petticoats, Aprons, Shoes, Stockings, Shifts, Caps, Tuscan Hats, a Bible, a Book of Common Prayer and the Whole Duty of Man.' Today, pupils at the school or those who are grant-aided, continue to be supported until their formal education is complete. So much for the girls, but what about the boys? Before 1717, when the United Grand Lodge of England was formed, both the Antients and the Moderns Grand Lodges acknowledged the need to feed, clothe, educate and train the sons of Freemasons. In 1798 the Junior Grand Warden of the Antients, William Burwood created a charity for that very purpose.

A similar charity was established by the Moderns seven years later at the suggestion of Sir Francis Columbine Daniel and members of the Royal Naval Lodge. An amazing character was Sir Francis, a doctor and apothecary; he was awarded the Royal Humane Society's special award for his invention of the inflatable lifejacket, which has since saved so many lives at sea. Sir Francis had one other claim to fame or should I say infamy: Allegedly, he was accidently knighted, when attending a Buckingham Palace garden party. Joining what he presumed was a queue to be presented; on bending his knee he was suddenly dubbed with the royal sword. Of course, once it had touched his shoulders, he could not be *unmade* - hence his honorific title.

The Union of the Two Grand Lodges took place in 1813, but it was not until three years later, that the two boy's charities were united as one, under the patronage of the Grand Master, the Duke of Sussex, but he was firmly against the provision of an actual school building as such. The policy of providing grants for clothing and education continued, but it was not until 1852 that a fund was initiated, once again by the Earl of Zetland, for a purpose built school constructed in Wood Green, North London, which eventually offered a basic education for 100 boys. The Royal Masonic Institution for Boys centenary was celebrated at the Albert Hall in 1898 and it was announced that over £140,000 had been raised, the largest total ever, towards the construction of a larger school at Bushey Grove in Hertfordshire, which was not completed until 1903. This new accommodation was sufficient for up to 400 pupils, but after the Second World War, it became less fashionable for children to be separated from their families in order to receive their early education and by 1977 the school was regrettably closed.

The principle however, of supporting the sons of Freemasons, with assistance and grants towards their education did not mean the end of the Royal Masonic Institution for Boys. In 1982 it was subsumed into the Masonic Trust for Girls and Boys, which in 2003 was granted use of the title, The Royal Masonic Trust for Girls and Boys by Her Majesty, Queen Elizabeth.

We now direct our attention to the Royal Masonic Benevolent Institution (otherwise referred to as the RMBI), and the vital part played at its inception by

Dr Robert Crucefix who, with the passing of the Poor Law in 1832, argued that elderly Freemasons, fallen on hard times, could end up in the workhouse, unless an appropriate fund was established for the provision of an Asylum scheme. Once again, it was the Duke of Sussex who argued against spending Masonic charity funds on buildings, rather than awarding grants to needy individuals.

The Duke of Sussex died in 1842, and it was Doctor Robert who initiated the building of the Asylum for Aged and Decayed Freemasons in Croydon two years later. Sadly, he died just a few months before the Asylum's opening in February 1850 and the formation of the RMBI in May of that year. It continued its function of providing either annuities or accommodation at the Croydon Asylum for over 100 years, after which the premises was taken over by Age Concern. In 1947, the first major building project containing self-contained flats and communal areas was launched at Harwood Court in Hove, Sussex. Since then the RMBI has built or acquired seventeen similar premises throughout England and Wales, including Zetland Court in Bournemouth.

Apart from caring for over a thousand Freemasons, their wives or widows in the previously mentioned residential homes, the RMBI currently supplies nursing care, dementia support, respite care and sheltered accommodation. It also helps to provide holidays and home improvement loans as well as annuities for those wishing to remain in their own homes.

Before we detail the excellent work of the New Masonic Samaritan Fund, perhaps we should remember that its original function as a Samaritan Fund was to provide assistance to those who sought treatment at the Royal Masonic Hospital, but were of insufficient means. The original Freemasons' War Hospital dated from the end of the First World War, when its promoters took a lease on the old London lying-in hospital in the Fulham Road, treating and rehabilitating many returning injured servicemen. Thus the idea of a Masonic Hospital gained impetus but it was not until 1933 that it was formally opened as the Royal Masonic Hospital by their Majesties, King George V and Queen Mary in Ravenscourt Park, West London.

Thereafter the excellent standards of treatment and aftercare were highly regarded throughout the medical profession. Indeed trainee nurses could find employment anywhere in the world and their special silver belt buckles became identified as a coveted honour. The hospital's remit was to offer treatment and aftercare at a reasonable cost, but could not provide free treatment for Freemasons and their dependents; however, during the Second World War, the hospital reverted to a war hospital, treating over 8,500 servicemen at no cost to the government. When the war ended many independent private hospitals were shut down, but the Royal Masonic Hospital was allowed to remain independent.

The formation of the New Masonic Samaritan Fund in 1990 with its own President and Governing Council resulted from the realisation that the Royal Masonic Hospital was not always the best place for patients to receive treatment, nor for their families to visit them. The Fund's scope was broadened so that assistance could be provided to ensure that treatment could take place at any local hospital providing the appropriate medical facilities both at a convenient time and cost. The fund works closely with Lodge Almoners, who provide an essential link with Lodge members.

It was Sir Arthur Bagnal, back in 1974, who proposed that changes should be made to the administration of Masonic Charities, particularly in view of the amalgamation of the Girls and Boys Schools. He advocated the formation of a new central charity called the Grand Charity, and in order for Lodges to respond to this, a new Lodge Officer was created – the Charity Steward. On 1st January 1981, the Board of Benevolence was officially replaced by the Grand Charity, a grant making body, overseeing contributions from Grand Lodge, English Lodges and individual Freemasons. Since then, it has provided a total of £80 million to thousands of petitioners and non-Masonic charities. Its grants cover three main areas:

- Masonic grants: Assisting Freemasons experiencing hardship with their families, including where necessary the provision of mobility equipment.
- Non-Masonic grants: Support for national charities, large and small, plus special provision for hospices and disaster relief worldwide, for example relief for the victims of Tsunamis and other natural disasters.
- Other Masonic Charities: Grants to any other Masonic Charities should the need arise.

So what has this lecture to do with Father Christmas? Surely it goes without saying that a Freemason's generosity extends beyond the collections of the Lodge Almoner and its Charity Steward, indeed also the Lodge itself. At the Festive Board raffle, every Freemason becomes Father Christmas, enabling a local charity to continue its good work, with a stocking full of members' contributions.

Finally, I am grateful to Worshipful Brother Ken Brown of Rottingdean Lodge No. 4961 for the following Masonic inspiration:

The Night before Christmas

Twas the night before Christmas and all through the house
Not a creature was stirring, not even a mouse;
The children were sleeping, so quiet and so simple,
And even their father was home from the Temple!
In bed, he was reading in manner habitual,
A particular part of his little blue Ritual -
His eyelids then drooped – and slowly they closed
And into the realms of slumber he dozed,
And as he quite happily started to snore,
He dreamt, such a dream as he'd not had before
He thought that he saw, o'er the rooftops on high,
A reindeer-drawn sleigh flying through the night sky!
The driver he knew in a moment, of course -

It was -Worshipful Brother Santa Claus!
Driving his reindeer above the snow,
With names the dreamer was certain to know -
'On, Warden! On, Deacon! and Treasurer true!
On, Master! On Tyler! and Inner Guard too!'
Then the sleigh came to rest, with a bump, on the tiles,
And Santa Claus entered the room, wreathed in smiles –
'Happy Christmas, my Brother!' cried out the good soul
And Greetings Fraternal - from the North Pole!
I'm here to fulfil my mission in life,
I've gifts for your children, and one for your wife!'
The dreamer accepted the presents with glee
Then said, 'Is there nought in your sack left for me?'
'Pray look, there may be a small gift inside -
T'would be gratefully received, and faithfully applied!'
Santa looked in his sack, but nothing he found -
He searched and he sought and he looked all around,
Then he smiled, and produced from a fold in his jacket
A small, but important and nice-looking packet:
'Here's your gift!' cried he, 'I felt sure I had one -
And it's just the thing for a Freemason!'
The dreamer then tore the wrappings asunder -
And looked at the present inside in wonder:
Just a small printed card was revealed to his eyes
Bearing the following brief message wise -
'Brotherly Love - is yours forever;
Relief, if you need it - and may you never -
And the Truth that has been decreed,
That being a Mason, you're rich indeed!'
The dreamer awoke! The room was bare
But there drifted back on the cold night air
A sound of bells - and a message of cheer -
'Joyous Noel! And a Prosperous New Year!'

References:

Albert Mackey, *Lexicon of Freemasonry*, Griffin, Bohn & Co, London 1861
Robert Freke Gould, *History of Freemasonry*, Thomas Jack, London 1887
Bernard Jones, *Freemason's Guide and Compendium*, George Harrap, London 1950
John Hamill, *Prestonian Lecture*, Lewis Masonic, Hersham 1993
The Independent, 7th May 1995
UGLE Library Charities Exhibition 2009 – Grand Lodge, Great Queen Street, London

CHAPTER FOUR

DARKNESS MUCH MORE VISIBLE

A dungeon horrible, on all sides round,
As one great furnace flamed, yet from those flames,
No light, but rather darkness visible
Served only to discover sights of woe.

THIS DESCRIPTION OF hell is from *Paradise Lost* by the great seventeenth-century poet, John Milton (1608-74) and predates our ceremony of raising by almost a century, but is it hell that the Worshipful Master has in mind when he says to the Third Degree Candidate:

> I will now beg you to observe that the light of a Master Mason is but darkness visible, serving only to express that gloom which rests on the prospect of eternity; it is that mysterious veil which the eye of human reason cannot penetrate, unless assisted by that light which is from above.

Before examining accusations of Masonic paganism in the book *Darkness Visible* by the Anglican clergyman, Walton Hannah, we perhaps need to understand what kind of light a Freemason experiences as *darkness visible*. When we close our eyes before going to sleep, dreams may well soon pervade our resting state, but those dreams generally depict imaginary activities not scenes of hell! Meanwhile, that temporary darkness brought about by lowering the eyelids in daytime cannot usually reveal any light of inspiration, which could otherwise have been obtained.

Perhaps the answer may lie with the Initiate's first encounter with the Lodge Tyler when hoodwinked and slip-shod. He will no doubt have been bemused by first emptying his pockets and removing one shoe, then having various parts of his body exposed. What is going on? After some loud door knocking, he is announced:

> Mr John Smith, a poor candidate in a state of darkness, who has been well and worthily recommended, regularly proposed and approved in open lodge, and now comes of his own free will and accord, properly prepared, humbly soliciting to be admitted to the mysteries and privileges of Freemasonry.

When asked how he hopes to obtain those privileges, the answer is, '…by the help of God, being free and of good report.' Very soon, he will be asked in all cases of difficulty and danger, in whom does he put his trust? 'God!' is of course the correct answer - and having found his faith so well founded he is then invited to follow his leader, '…with a firm but humble confidence, for where the name of God is invoked, we trust no danger can ensue.' After several perambulations the Candidate finds himself kneeling down and repeating an obligation with one hand apparently resting on the Volume of the Sacred Law. He is finally asked the predominant wish of his heart, which unsurprisingly turns out to be light and the Holy Bible is focused as his primary visual encounter.

Thus for the first five or six minutes of his experience with Freemasonry, his faith in the Great Architect of the Universe predetermines the trust in those he cannot see, whether that God is called; Allah, Yahweh or anything else. It is that trust, which we may well regard as the *light* of Freemasonry. In his book *The Meaning of Masonry* written in 1932, W. L. Wilmshurst observes that there are two paths open to the Candidate, 'a path of light and a path of darkness.'

When placed in the North East corner he is intended to see that on one side of him is the path that leads to the perpetual light of the East, into which he is encouraged to proceed, and that on the other is that of spiritual obscurity and ignorance into which it is possible for him to remain or relapse.

It is a parable of the dual paths of life open to each one of us. On the one hand the path of selfishness, material desires and sensual indulgence, of intellectual blindness and moral stagnation. On the other the path of moral and spiritual progress, in pursuing which one may decorate and adorn the Lodge within him with the ornaments and jewels of grace and with the invaluable furniture of true knowledge, and which he may dedicate, in all his actions to the service of God and of his fellow men.

In 1957, in his book: *The Ceremony of Initiation*, Wilmshurst also claims that throughout Masonic Ritual, by the word *light* we must understand *consciousness*. Therefore, 'Let there be light' really implies, 'let there be a quickening, heightening and expansion of consciousness in that which has hitherto been unconscious, or but limitedly conscious.'

Some measure of consciousness is present in everything, in every kingdom of Nature, from mineral to man. In man is gathered up the consciousness of all the sub-human kingdoms, and in him that consciousness is capable of being advanced still farther; indeed, to a stage beyond the human. In 1962 the Reverend Walton Hannah published *Darkness Visible*, a sceptical account of Freemasonry reflecting the controversy aroused by the Anglican Bishop of Southwark, Dr. Mervyn Stockwood. The Bishop banned non-Christian Masonic church services in his diocese, on the basis that, '...as long as Masonry exists as a secret society with a religious ritual, it will excite curiosity and questioning.'

Walton Hannah was an Anglican clergyman who displayed a very deep distrust of every religion not his own. Catholicism comes in for some cheap shots in the book, which is very strange, as by the time of his death he had become a Catholic priest. He was well known for hiding his identity and corresponding with Freemasons, some of who actually thought he was a member. He also built up a very large library of Masonic titles available to non-Masons to learn about Freemasonry.

In his preface the author pays tribute to a '...certain Bishop and Past Grand Chaplain, whom I will not embarrass by naming' for his sympathetic understanding and courtesy in offering so much of his valuable time to trying, at the authors request, to persuade him '...to a different opinion on Freemasonry.' The Bishop succeeded in convincing him of the personal sincerity of the individual Christian Freemason, '...which nowhere in these pages do I wish to impugn.' He opens with the statement that:

> ...as Freemasonry very considerably overlaps with the non-Roman Churches, particularly with the Church of England, my concern is rather to examine the extent to which this overlap is morally and theologically justified.

In other words, he inquires whether Freemasonry is compatible with the light of Christianity.

The author may have found some of his initial investigations limited by a lack of information, because of the secrecy surrounding the craft at that time, although even by 1918, in his *New Encyclopaedia of Freemasonry* the writer, Arthur Edward Waite suggested that, '...it is common knowledge that the secrets have been betrayed times out of number and it is too honest to insert the usual Masonic qualifications of alleged or supposed disclosures.'

Waite goes onto suggest that the real secret of Masonry is not a secret at all, but rather a *mystery*, verbally incommunicable to the outsider and Mason alike, the Masonic life based on moral symbolism and allegory, which the initiate, having been given the ceremonial key, must discover for himself.

However, our author is quite clear about his position on Masonic secrecy and admits his conviction that for a Christian to pledge himself to a religious organisation which offers prayer and worship to God, which deliberately excludes the name of '... our Lord and Saviour Jesus Christ, in whose name only is salvation to be found', is apostolic. Mind you, he does accept that there are many Christians who are also Masons who do not see it in that light, either because they do not take their ritual very seriously, or because they allow other considerations such as the good works, benevolence and moral uprightness of the Craft, to outweigh the clearly pagan implications of its formulae.

At this point, it must be emphasised that he appears to ignore the universal nature of Freemasonry, membership of which is offered to all believers in a supreme being, by whichever name that being is referred. A Muslim initiate would be welcome to complete his obligation on the Holy Qur'an, while aspiring Jewish members would also need to put on their skullcaps and their hand on the Torah. The resultant camaraderie is particularly due to the common belief and mutual acceptance among members of the Craft. However, Walton Hannah argues that Masonry is not so much a religion as a parasite on religion, and a rival to the Church as a moral guide.

Furthermore he believes that there are in Masonic workings distinct elements of religion in a far more supernatural sense of the word, a religion that is entirely non-Christian. Although, he does admit that Masonic ritual is worked in the spirit of a solemn religious ceremony; it is customary to sing hymns at the opening and closing of the Lodge, candles are lighted beside the three pedestals, and the Bible is traditionally open in front of the Worshipful Master. The Lodge is always opened and closed with prayer, which is also offered for the candidate at his initiation, passing and raising.

The Grand or Royal sign is accompanied by the exclamation: 'All glory to the Most High' and most Lodges have Chaplains and Organists who play a regular part in the ceremonies. Meanwhile Masonry claims to imbue its initiates with a spiritual and esoteric light. Indeed at the moment he replies that the predominant wish of his heart is light, the hoodwink is removed to a thunderous hand clap from the assembled Brethren and he becomes aware of his Lodge surroundings for the first time. The six Emblematic Lights of Freemasonry are immediately brought to his attention, beginning with the Volume of the Sacred Law.

Still on the subject of light, the author regards the religious outlook of Masonry as an echo of eighteenth-century Deism, in stressing the light of nature as a moral guide, in beginning and ending with man's aspirations to God, with man's justifying himself in the eyes of God by his own good works.

Although Masonry also echoes Gnosticism in claiming to impart an esoteric light disdaining any conception of God reaching down from Heaven to save and heal mankind, Christianity is a faith revealed by God to man, not a system worked out by man of ascent to God. He then goes on to deplore the treatment of Bishops and other clergy, who undergo what he describes as a rather ludicrous humiliation during their introduction to Masonry, whereby a Bishop would experience a rather ludicrous humiliation during the preparation for initiation.

In the name of the Great Architect of the universe, a Bishop should be deprived of his Episcopal ring and pectoral cross along with other articles of metal and be blindfolded, haltered and partially undressed in search of a Masonic light of which the Church in her fullness of grace knows nothing. It is an act of humility to a purely human institution, which seems to differ not only in degree but also in kind from a layman undergoing the same ceremony. What he chooses to disregard (or conveniently forget) is that the Bishop is treated no differently from a member of the Royal Family, such as the Duke of Kent, who no doubt underwent his initiation with the same sense of humiliation as the rest of us, to emphasise the egalitarian nature of the Craft. After all, when being presented to the Duke at a Masonic function, there would be no need in theory for anyone to bow or kneel. Instead, one's hand would be offered with the words, 'Welcome Brother!'

Meanwhile, we are reminded that in contrast to the secretive nature of Freemasonry, the teachings of the Church are public property, which are openly and fearlessly proclaimed before the world. They have been for centuries examined, criticised, attacked, and subjected to every test and scrutiny known to the scholar, friendly or hostile. The clergy have familiarised themselves with popular objections to creed, sacraments and service books, and should have a clear answer to them. Freemasonry, on the other hand, although sometimes denounced, has been completely immune from real criticism and investigation from the outside.

The average Mason has seen no necessity to examine his workings critically or to justify them from the Christian point of view to the world outside. Why should he bother to find answers to questions that he is oath-bound not to answer? If Freemasonry claims to possess secrets the knowledge of which would benefit all mankind in enabling a man to lead a higher and more moral life, it is immoral to keep that knowledge to itself. But if Freemasonry does not possess such secrets, it is equally immoral for it to claim that it does in fact possess them.

To be fair, the author then moves onto the areas of benevolence, brotherhood and tolerance, admitting that Masons are indeed generous with a lavishness, which often leaves Christian giving far behind. The Charity column, which circulates at the festive board, often returns with more paper than silver in it than the average collection at Evensong. Let us also remember that Masonic institutions, their hospital for sick Masons, their nursing home, and their schools for the children of Masons are efficiently run. They have a fund of benevolence for the benefit of poor and distressed Masons, their widows and orphans. In addition to these closed shop charities and other deserving non-Masonic institutions, Masonic Lodges liberally support Lord Mayor Appeals and so on.

Undoubtedly however, the greatest attraction of Freemasonry to most of its adherents is not its ritual or religious implications, nor its supposed advantages in business and certain professions, but the warm fellowship of sincere and genuine friendliness and Brotherhood at Lodge meetings and at after-proceedings, what the Greeks call a *koinonia* or communion by intimate participation, which has to be experienced to be fully appreciated. Indeed, no one would wish to level any criticism against this were not Masons inclined a little self-righteously to hold themselves up as an example to the Church in claiming to have achieved Brotherhood and mutual love where the Church has failed. The Reverend C. K. Hughes, signing himself 'Priest and Freemason' wrote in the *Guardian* (Feb 23, 1951):

> Proctors in convocation should ask themselves why so many elements of fellowship, loyalty, brotherhood, charity and the like, which marked the New Testament Church are absent from the Church of England, but supposed to be present in Freemasonry?

It is still believed that the Roman Catholic Church has condemned Freemasonry, and that any Roman Catholic on initiation becomes excommunicated. Contrary to popular rumour, it does not give dispensations for converted Masons to continue in Masonry. This condemnation is resented by Grand Lodge Masons of the English-speaking world.

It is popularly felt to be unjust, and the belief is widespread that all Papal condemnations, in so far as they include all Masonic systems, are based on a complete misunderstanding of what Grand Lodge Masonry really stands for. It is commonly thought by Masons that the Roman Catholic objections to Freemasonry are in some way bound up with the confessional, that there must be no secrets, which could be withheld from the confessor.

This is not so. A Catholic is as entitled to his secrets, provided they are not sinful, as anyone else. Four groups of Presbyterians and one group of Methodists have pronounced against Freemasonry. The *Original Secession* in Scotland repudiated Freemasonry as early as 1757, on the grounds that it was against the moral law to bind oneself by oath to secrets, which were not revealed till afterwards.

The Presbyterian Church of Ireland makes abstention from Freemasonry a condition of membership. The Free Presbyterian Church of Scotland imposed a similar condition of membership in 1927. The Orthodox Presbyterian Church of America set up a Committee on Secret Societies, which condemned Masonry, mainly on the grounds of religious indifferentism. The English Methodists passed a resolution on Freemasonry in 1927, claiming that the Christian message of salvation through faith in Christ is wholly incompatible with the claims, which have been put forward by Freemasons. The American Lutherans have also strongly condemned Freemasonry. The Missouri Synod for instance, holds that, '…these organisations, which our Church terms 'Lodges' demand a belief in God, but not in the God and Father of our Lord Jesus Christ.'

Their rituals often provide for an oath, which a Christian cannot but regard as unnecessary or even frivolous and blasphemous. Such rituals oftentimes promote salvation by the Law and by good works, not by faith in Jesus Christ. These organisations most frequently claim to be non-sectarian and to allow for complete religious freedom. Nevertheless their rituals disregard, level out, or even deny the most precious truths of the Christian faith in order to make their moral and religious principles acceptable to anyone joining the organisation regardless of his religious convictions. The author sums up his treatise on *Darkness Visible* by suggesting that these Protestant bodies represent minorities and are therefore unimportant. Take them together with the vast Roman Catholic and Eastern Orthodox communions however, and it will be evident that the majority of Christians throughout the world have condemned Freemasonry as incompatible with the claims of our Lord and Saviour.

Finally, one startling fact emerges, which should make the Christian Mason more than a little thoughtful, 'No Church that has seriously investigated the religious teachings and implications of Freemasonry has ever yet failed to condemn it.' Is the Church of England too mortally involved to speak her mind? This thought provoking *Revelation and Interpretation of Freemasonry* merely occupies the first 70 pages. Part Two then devotes the next 150 pages in fine detail to a significant amount of our Masonic Rituals including the First, Second and Third degrees, together with the relevant Tracing Boards and the Installation of the Worshipful Master.

It then focuses on the Royal Arch in similar detail. Finally, a number of Appendices describe other Masonic Degrees including Mark, Knights Templar, Allied and the Ancient and Accepted Rite. It's as if the author feels that the man in the street who is blind to the secrets of Masonry needs a light to appreciate exactly what is involved in the initiation ceremony, and exactly what his oath represents. From my own perspective, the light of Freemasonry offers hope and companionship to those who believe in a Supreme Being.

By way of conclusion, after going blind, John Milton also wrote the poem *On his blindness*. In the sonnet's last line; he reflects in common with Freemasons today, that even with his disability he still has a valued place in the world:

When I consider how my light is spent
Ere half my days in this dark world and wide,
And that one talent which is death to hide
Lodged with me useless, though my soul more bent
To serve there with my Maker, and present
My true account, lest He returning chide,
'Doth God exact day-labour, light denied?'
I fondly ask. But patience, to prevent
That murmur, soon replies, 'God doth not need
Either man's work or his own gifts. Who best
Bear his mild yoke, they serve him best. His state
is Kingly: thousands at his bidding speed,
And post o'er land and ocean without rest;
they also serve who only stand and wait.

References:

A. E. Waite, *New Encyclopaedia of Freemasonry*, Rider & Co. London 1918

W. L. Wilmshurst, *Meaning of Masonry*, Rider and Co. London 1932

Walton Hannah, *Darkness Visible*, Augustine Press, London 1952

W. L. Wilmshurst, *The Ceremony of Initiation*, Rider & Co, London 1957

CHAPTER FIVE

2ND DUKE OF RICHMOND - GRAND MASTER
1724-1725

7th Duke of Richmond
*(Reproduced by kind permission of Martin Cherry,
Library and Museum of Freemasonry, London)*

THE INSPIRATION FOR this chapter comes from having a once-removed relationship with the current Tenth Duke of Richmond, in that my wife, while Chief Executive of Chichester Counselling services, was invited on several occasions to take tea with him at Goodwood House, being as he was the Charity's Patron.

It was the Seventh Duke however, as Sussex Provincial Grand Master from 1901 to 1925, who inspired the naming of a newly consecrated Craft and Mark Lodge, plus a Royal Arch Chapter. Styled Lord Settrington from birth, he was born at Portland

Place, London, the eldest son of Charles Henry Gordon-Lennox, Sixth Duke of Richmond and Frances Harriett, daughter of Algernon Frederick Greville. He was educated at Eton between 1859 and 1863, after which he joined the Grenadier Guards. In 1860 he became known as the Earl of March after his father succeeded in the Dukedom. Charles married firstly Amy Mary, daughter of Percy Ricardo, of Bramley Park, Guildford, Surrey.

They had three sons and two daughters. After her death in August 1879, aged 30, he then married Isabel Sophie, daughter of William George Craven, in 1882. They had two daughters. His second wife Isabel died in November 1887, aged 24. The Duke remained a widower until his death in January 1928, aged 82. He retired in 1869 after being elected Member of Parliament for West Sussex. The Duke represented that constituency until it was abolished for the 1885 General Election, when he was returned to the House of Commons for the Chichester Constituency. He held his seat until 1889, soon after which he and his brother, Lord Algernon Gordon-Lennox volunteered to serve in the Second South African Boer War.

It was back in 1877, that he was initiated into the Lodge of Union No. 38 in Chichester. Twenty-four years later in 1901, he became Right Worshipful Grand Master for the Province of Sussex. On 27th September 1903, Gordon-Lennox succeeded his father as Seventh Duke of Richmond and Lennox and 2nd Duke of Gordon. In 1904, King Edward VII made him a Knight Grand Cross of the Royal Victorian Order of the Garter. The Duke would be succeeded by his eldest son, Charles. His second son Lord Esmé Gordon-Lennox rose to Brigadier-General in the British Army, while his third and youngest son Lord Bernard Gordon-Lennox also became a Major in the Army.

It was in 1901, while still the Earl of March, he became Provincial Grand Master, continuing as the Duke of Richmond until 1925. It was on the 22nd March 1906 that he presided at the Consecration of the Sussex Masonic Lodge No. 3143, which still bears his name today. In 1936, the number 3143 was also attached to the Duke of Richmond Royal Arch Chapter, but it was not until 1945 however, that the Sussex Mark Lodge No. 1025 was consecrated bearing the same name.

Now our attention must focus on Charles Lennox, the Second Duke of Richmond (1701-1750) the only son of the first Duke and the main subject of this chapter. His interest in Freemasonry was unfortunately transitory, being a man of so many passionate interests as will be shortly revealed. Until he succeeded his father in 1723, he was simply titled the Earl of March. His early years were spent quietly and happily with his family and he was privately educated. His marriage at the age of 18 was apparently arranged in 1719 to settle a gambling debt incurred by his father, and his bride Sarah, the daughter of the Earl of Cadogan was only 13 at the time.

He immediately set out on the Grand Tour of Holland, France, Austria and Italy for the next three years, during which time his young bride was sent home to live with

The most Noble PRINCE CHARLES DUKE of RICHMOND, LENOX, and AUBIGNY, &c.&c.
Who Died Aug.t 8th 1750. Ætat. 49
From an Original Picture Prepared by His Grace, to the Corporation of the CITY of CHICHESTER.
Published by Geo. Smith, Painter at CHICHESTER.

2nd Duke of Richmond
(Charles II, Duke of Richmond – engraving by William Smith c. 1750 –
Reproduced by kind permission of West Sussex Record Office)

her parents. Bearing in mind that his tenure as Grand Master was to begin in 1724, his return to England occurred in 1722, when his marriage was successfully resumed, and its long lasting security and happiness is testified in many family letters, which have survived to this day. That same year the Earl joined the Army and in September he became a Captain in the Royal Regiment of Horse Guards. Also in that year he became the M.P. for Chichester, but on 2nd May 1723, his father died at Goodwood and he adopted the title and responsibilities of the Second Duke of Richmond.

His influence spread to many neighbouring constituencies, and in the 1734 election the Duke unsuccessfully attempted to gain a seat in New Shoreham, a venal borough, which he once described as '...a new whore that was anybody's for their money'. Despite this setback he eventually became Mayor of Chichester in 1735. If that were not all, the Duke was also particularly interested in medicine, science and antiquity and became a Fellow of the Royal Society in February 1724. He was awarded a Doctorate in Law at Cambridge University in 1728 and in that same year he was elected a fellow of the Royal College of Physicians. Also much later in 1741 the Duke was to become President of the London Hospital.

Like many members of the eighteenth-century aristocracy, the Duke was a devotee of opera. He was elected a Governor of the Royal Academy of Music on 30th November 1725, and among his papers is an autograph list of persons willing to subscribe £200 to the Corporation of the Royal Academy of Music towards putting on operas, beginning in 1728. It was opera, which introduced the Duke to the impresario and art dealer, Owen MacSwinney, an employee of the Academy from 1724. He toured Italy looking for singers and scores for the Duke and managed to commission a number of paintings, twelve of which still hang in the Great Dining Room at Goodwood.

In 1732, when workmen discovered the famous Neptune and Minerva Stone while digging foundations for the new Council Chamber in North Street, Chichester, it was presented to the Duke, who had it transported to Goodwood. The Duke became a Fellow of the Society of Antiquaries in April 1736 and actively supported the investigation of ancient relics. In 1746, the Duke paid for the restoration of the Market Cross in Chichester and in 1750 he presented to the Society of Antiquaries a drawing of a piece of Roman pavement found in the Bishop's Garden in Chichester.

We now turn to the Duke's Army record, which is particularly relevant at this point, for on April 8th 1724, the very year that he became Right Worshipful Grand Master, he was appointed Aide-de-Camp to King George I, a position which was confirmed by King George II on his accession. The Duke became a Brigadier General in July 1739 and a Major General in June 1742. In 1743, he accompanied the King throughout his European campaign, being responsible, as His Majesty's Master of the Horse, for a baggage train of 662 horses and took part in the Battle of Dettingen.

He was created Lieutenant General in June 1745 and full General in the same November. The Duke was given command of the forces which faced the Scottish Jacobites in their Southerly march, and when they finally turned back after reaching Derby, he chased the retreating army as far as Carlisle, before returning to his Sussex estate, pleased that he had rid the country of a Scottish invasion. This was to lead to the office, which would ultimately give him most pleasure. In February 1750 he was appointed Colonel of the Royal Horse Guards, and thereby became reunited with many officers with which he shared his youth. Thankfully, we are able to gain a valuable insight into his activities on the battlefield around that time, due to his regular correspondence with the Duke of Newcastle - in all over 450 letters from 1724 to 1750, which survive to this day. Sadly, time prevents us from examining any more than just one of his letters, written from King George's quarters at Biberich, on the right bank of the River Rhine, near Mainz on the 21st August 1743:

My Dear Lord,

I wrote a very long letter to your Grace by the last Messager, butt as he call'd upon me in a hurry I was forced to leave off very abruptly, which was very lucky for you, as the letter was at least long enough as it was. I thinke the last toppick was that of Mr Pelham's having had no answer from your brother Secretary here & I don't find he has sent any yett:

Monsr Freechappell does nothing now butt the part of a head groom, that is in taking care of all his Hanover horses, & I do all the functions of the Master of the Horse, that is helping him into his voiture, & setting in it by him & so forth, butt have nothing to do with his Hanover horses, nor voitures, only the privilege of going in them, butt the greasing of the wheels & all that is entirely under Monsr Freechappell. So you see I have Cloake enough to cover my discontents

I thinke I should have some merit with him in my private station, butt then thinke of that day, & that the King's Master of the Horse must have been that day on foot, if Generall Honeywood had not been so kind as to lend him a horse. I own the reflection of it shocks me. Butt I never have mentioned it to any body butt the Duchess of Richmond & yourself, the two best friends I thinke I have in the world, there can be no excuse for it butt the yellow sash, However, without bragging I believe I may say that it was the King of England & not the Elector of Hanover that beat the French that day.

I had the advantage to see as much as any one man could see of the whole affair; After it was over, I went up to his Majesty, had the honour to dine with him, upon the field of battle, & after he had got into his voiture, he did the honor to aske me if I would go in his chaise; upon which not a little in the Falstaf stile I rub'd my face and said I was so hott with the heat of the day, that I rather chose to ride, for God knows I was as cool as a cucumber.

I must now tell you with a most sincere concern that he has been very much out of order, his old complaint of the piles has been stop'd, which threw him into a violent purging, that weeekn'd him to a terribel degree, then when that stop'd, he had a swell'd and painefull leg, which must not be call'd the gout. That's gon off, & now it is in his eyes, one of them particularly extreamly bad, however he goes out every day & looks pretty well.

You will hear by post at least of our scituation, if not 'tis soon told. The Austrians are on the other side having pass'd over our own bridge. Prince Charles has collected his whole army together between Frybourg and Brisack, in order to make a puch a cross the Rhine, butt Monsr Maurice de Saxe with 8 or 9000 men has Cottoned him all the way from before Strasbourg, so there certainly will be some bloody noses there. I am quite in love with Prince Charles, he is to the full as agreeable as his brother & surely he has great military merit. This is a tedious letter, butt it's your own fault, for having given me so much encouragement. My love to dear Mr Pelham, & be assured my Dearest Lord, that I am forever your grace's faithfull & obliged.

RICHMOND, &C.

Back home in England, his local prestige and power led the Duke to mount a campaign against Sussex smugglers, which in the 1740's was described as:

…a guerrilla war between the smugglers and the officers of government'. A conflict between '…an organised resistance to the government, in which towns were besieged, battles fought, Customs Houses burnt down and the greatest atrocities committed.

The Duke resolved to capture and convict smugglers in order to stop smuggling in Sussex completely. He was incensed by the atrocious murder of William Galley, a Customs House Officer, and Daniel Chater, a shoemaker by fourteen notorious smugglers, seven of which were caught and he saw executed at Chichester.

In 1746, the Duke received a letter from his friend Tom Hill, which suggested that the Venetian artist Canaletto wished to be presented, '…and that it might be a good idea to let him draw a view of the river from your dining room.'

The two pictures, *The Thames from Richmond House* and *Whitehall from Richmond House* still hang at Goodwood today. Talking of Goodwood, it would perhaps be an appropriate final gesture to mention the Duke's fascination with collecting wild animals from all over the world, many of which were provided by his overseas diplomatic associates. The Duke's zoological collection apparently included:

5 wolves, 2 tygers, 1 lyon, a jackall, 2 lepers, 1 sived cat, 3 small monkeys, 1 large monkey, 3 foxes, 2 greenland dogs, 3 vulturs, 2 eagles, 1 kite, 2 owls, 1 armadilla, 3 bears, 3 racoons, a woman tyger, 1 pecaverre, and 7 caswarris.

Old Daimlers and Bugatis – eat your heart out!

References:

R. F. Gould, *History of Freemasonry,* Thomas Jack, London 1886

B. E. Jones, *Freemason's Guide and Compendium*, George Harrap, London 1950

T. J. McCann, *Correspondence of the Dukes of Richmond and Newcastle*, Alan Sutton, Glos. 1983

CHAPTER SIX

FREEMASONRY AND THE BIBLE

FOR GOD SAID: 'In strength will I establish this mine house to stand firm forever.'

As there is no biblical evidence to support that fundamental Masonic statement, this chapter hopes to explore both the literal and symbolic relevance of the Bible in Freemasonry. Every Freemason, throughout the world will certainly recall the first question asked when he expressed an initial interest in joining our unique Brotherhood, 'Do you believe in a supreme being?' At that point his proposer would doubtless have explained that that an obligation would need to be taken by every candidate, with the right hand resting on the Bible, and to further explain that without his reverence for such a Holy Book, there was nothing, which might otherwise convince the Brethren of his sincerity. It would also have been pointed out that although in this country the volume in question would normally be the Holy Bible, in other parts of the world it could easily be replaced by say, the Holy Qur'an or Torah, depending on the candidate's particular religion. Nevertheless, once taken, a Freemason's obligation is binding upon him so long as he should live.

From the very outset the candidate is reminded with the prayer that:

> ...this candidate for Freemasonry, may so dedicate and devote his life to thy service as to become a true and faithful Brother among us. Endue him with a competency of thy Divine Wisdom, so that, assisted by the secrets of our Masonic art, he may the better be enabled to unfold the beauties of true Godliness to the honour and glory of Thy Holy Name.

If this were not all, he is soon questioned by the Worshipful Master: 'In all cases of difficulty and danger, in whom do you put your trust?'

Once he has affirmed that his trust is in God, he is assured that with his faith so well founded, he may rise and safely follow his leader with a firm but humble confidence, '...for where the name of God is invoked, we trust no danger will ensue.'

Later, during his initiation, it should come as no surprise that having ascertained that the predominant wish of his heart is *Light*, the moment immediately after that blessing is restored, his head is deliberately held down by the Junior Deacon, so that his very first visual contact with Freemasonry is the Volume of the Sacred Law, the most important of those Three Great Lights. Likewise, at the conclusion of the ceremony, the importance of the Bible is once again drawn to his attention in the charge:

> As a Freemason, I would first recommend to your most serious contemplation, the Volume of the Sacred Law, charging you to consider it as the unerring standard of truth and justice, and to regulate your action by the Divine precepts

it contains, therein you will be taught the important duties you owe to God, to your neighbour and to yourself.

Finally, the importance of the spiritual nature of his initiation may be emphasised via the Lecture on the First Degree Tracing Board; in particular the significance of Jacob's ladder:

> The covering of a Freemason's Lodge is a celestial canopy of divers colours, even the heavens. The way by which we, as Freemasons, hope to arrive there is by the assistance of a ladder, in scripture called Jacob's ladder. It has many staves or rounds, which point out as many moral virtues. The three principal ones are Faith, Hope and Charity; Faith in the Grand Architect of the Universe, Hope in Salvation, and to be in Charity with all men.
>
> This ladder, which reaches to the heavens, rests on the Volume of the Sacred law, because by the doctrines contained in that Holy Book, we are taught to believe in the wise dispensation of Divine providence; which belief, strengthens our Faith and enables us to ascend the first step. This Faith, naturally creates in us a Hope of becoming partakers of the blessed promises therein recorded, which Hope enables us to ascend the second step.
>
> But the third and last, being Charity, comprehends the whole, and the Freemason who is in possession of this virtue in its most ample sense, may justly be deemed to have attained the summit of his profession, figuratively speaking, an ethereal mansion, veiled from mortal eyes by the starry firmament, emblematically depicted in our Lodges by seven stars, which have an allusion to as many regularly made Freemasons, without which number no Lodge is perfect, nor can any candidate be legally initiated into the Order.

The attributes of Faith, Hope and Charity having been clearly emphasised, the initiate may perhaps recall the words of St Paul in his poignant Epistle to the Corinthians (*I Corinthians* 13:1):

> Though I speak with the tongues of men and of angels, and have not charity, I am become as sounding brass or a tinkling cymbal. And though I have the gift of prophecy and understanding all mysteries and all knowledge; and though I have all faith, so that I could remove mountains, and have not charity, I am nothing. And though I bestow all my goods to feed the poor, and though I give my body to be burned, and have not charity, it profiteth me nothing.
>
> Charity suffereth long and is kind; charity envieth not; charity vaunted not itself, is not puffed up, doth not behave itself unseemly, seeketh not her own, is not easily provoked, thinketh no evil; rejoiceth not in iniquity, but rejoiceth in the Truth; beareth all things, believeth all things, hopeth all

things, endureth all things. Charity never faileth; but whether there be prophecies, they shall fail; whether there be tongues, they shall cease; whether there be knowledge, it shall vanish away. For we know in part, and we prophesy in part. But when that which is perfect is come, then that which is in part shall be done away.

When I was a child, I spake as a child, I thought as a child; but when I became a man, I put away childish things. For now we see through a glass darkly; but then face to face; now I know in part; but then shall I know even as I am known. And now abideth faith, hope and charity, these three, but the greatest of these is charity.

At a significant point in the Entered Apprentice's passing to the Second Degree he is introduced to the hailing sign, or sign of perseverance, which allegedly took its rise from the time when Joshua fought the battles of the Lord, 'For it was in this position, he prayed fervently to the almighty to continue the light of day, that he might complete the overthrow of his enemies.'

To be a little more accurate, the King James Bible fails to mention any particular hand gestures in Joshua, Chapter 10, but certainly verifies the following:

Then spake Joshua to the Lord in the day when the Lord delivered up the Amorites before the children of Israel, and he said in the sight of Israel: Sun, stand thou still upon Gibeon; and thou, Moon, in the valley of Ajalon. And the Sun stood still, and the moon stayed until the people had avenged themselves upon their enemies.

Later, the Second Degree Tracing Board lecture offers a Fellow Craft the opportunity to consider another Bible story, found in Judges 12:4:

Now Jephthah gathered together all the men of Gilead and fought against Ephraim. And the men of Gilead defeated Ephraim, because they said, 'You Gileadites are fugitives of Ephraim among the Ephraimites and among the Manassites.' The Gileadites seized the fords of the Jordan before the Ephraimites arrived. And when any Ephraim who escaped said, 'Let me cross over,' the men of Gilead would say to him, 'Are you an Ephraim?' If he said, 'No,' then they would say to him, 'Then say, 'Shibboleth!' And he would say, 'Sibboleth,' for he could not pronounce it right. Then they would take him and kill him at the fords of the Jordan. There fell at that time forty-two thousand Ephraimites.

(In the Bible, the word *shibboleth* means either *an ear of grain* or *a flowing stream*, though constant Masonic use has contracted its meaning to 'an ear of corn near to a fall of water.')

In the Second and Third Degree ceremonies the candidate will be further spiritually prepared, and will be reminded by the Chaplain of our awareness of the Deity, whose name he invokes at each of the opening and closings. In his progression through the Three Degrees of Freemasonry, a candidate undertakes a journey of discovery, not only about himself, but also about the origins of our distinguished Order. He is invited to make a daily advancement in Masonic knowledge and his attention is drawn to the building of King Solomon's Temple, and the essential part played by our Master Hiram Abif, learning along the way that by his untimely death the genuine secrets of a Master Mason were *lost*.

Solomon's Kingdom stretched from the banks of the Euphrates right down to the Egyptian border. His immense power and wisdom were only superseded by his wealth and munificence. But his prime legacy was of course the Temple at Jerusalem, on which much of our ritual is based: As we read in 2 Chronicles 2:1:

> And Solomon determined to build an house for the name of the Lord, and an house for his kingdom. And Solomon told out threescore and ten thousand men to bear burdens, and fourscore thousand to hew in the mountain, and three thousand and six hundred to oversee them.
>
> And Solomon sent to Huram, the King of Tyre, saying: As thou didst deal with David, my father, and didst send him cedars to build him an house to dwell therein, even so deal with me. Behold, I build an house to the name of the Lord my God, to dedicate it to him, and to burn before him sweet incense, and for the continual showbread, and for the burnt offerings morning and evening. On the Sabbaths, and on the new moons, and on the solemn feasts of the Lord our God. This is an ordinance forever to Israel.

The appearance of Hiram Abif at Jerusalem is not chronicled specifically, although Solomon's request describes someone whose skills as a master craftsman leave little to the imagination:

> Send me now therefore a man cunning to work in gold, and in silver, and in brass, and in iron, and in purple and crimson, and blue, and that can skill to grave with the cunning men that are with me in Judah and in Jerusalem, whom David my father did provide.
>
> Send me also cedar trees, fir trees; and algum trees, out of Lebanon; for I know thy servants can skill to cut timber in Lebanon; and behold my servants shall be with thy servants, even to prepare me timber in abundance; for the house which I am about to build shall be wonderful great.

Under King Solomon, Israel attained its maximum glory. In fact some sections of Kings and Chronicles in the Bible almost read like a fairy story, but recent excavations prove that Israel's wealth and influence were grounded in reality, as in this passage from I Kings 4:1:

So King Solomon was King over all Israel ...and Solomon had 40,000 stalls of horses for his chariots and 12,000 horsemen' and later 'And Solomon built all the cities of store and cities for his chariots and cities for his horsemen.

We appear to have learned from the Phoenicians that Hiram Abif, a craftsman from Tyre who was responsible for the casting of the Temple furnishings was also entrusted with building Solomon's Navy:

> Although there were great forests in the neighbourhood of this place (which was Eloth on the Gulf of Akabah) the wood was not suitable for building purposes so Hiram had to transport all the timber needed to build ten ships on the backs of 8,000 camels.

Solomon was not slow to exploit foreign brains and labour: he even employed Phoenicians to captain his ships and to bring back the gold from Ophir, which is believed to have been Somaliland. And Solomon, by commanding nearly all the trade routes of the then known world, was also a captain of commerce. Again, we read in I Kings, Chapter 10:

> ...and Solomon had horses brought out of Egypt and linen yarn... and so for all the Kings of the Hittites and for the King of Syria did they bring them out by their means. Also – Now the weight of gold that came to Solomon in one year was six hundred threescore and six talents of gold.

(This equates to roughly 14 million pounds sterling at the present price of gold) Then there were the famous incense caravans from Arabia, which brought spices, gold and precious stones 1,250 miles to Israel. It was Arabian traders who told the Queen of Sheba about King Solomon, and prompted her famous association with him, which is recorded not only in Kings and Chronicles but in the Holy Qur'an as well. The reign of Solomon was indeed prosperous, and was not limited solely to Solomon's great court. Wealthy Israelites were fond of wearing clothing dyed red and blue and purple, obtained mainly from Hebron, which archaeologists have found to be the centre of the dye industry; dyeing vats were discovered there, with great stone basins fitted with inflow and outflow pipes.

There is evidence that Solomon was interested in botany and natural history. In the *Book of Kings* (I Kings 4:33) we read, '...and he spake of trees from the cedar tree that is in Lebanon even unto the Hyssop that springeth out of the wall: he spake also of beasts and of fowl and of creeping things and of fishes.'

But Solomon's wisdom is the characteristic for which he is best known. This is of course exemplified in the Judgement of Solomon:

Then came there two women that were harlots, unto the King... and the one woman said, O my Lord, I and this woman dwell in one house; and I was delivered of a child with her in the house. And it came to pass the third day after that I was delivered, that this woman was delivered also; and we were together; there was no stranger with us in the house, save we two in the house. And this woman's child died in the night; because she overlaid it. (Perhaps this is the first recorded case of accidental smothering) ...and she arose at midnight, and took my son from beside me, while thy handmaid slept, and laid it in her bosom, and laid her dead child in my bosom.

The outcome of this story is well known:

...and the King said, Bring me a sword. And they brought a sword before the King. And the King said, divide the living child in two, and give half to the one and half to the other. Then spake the woman who's the living child was unto the King...O my Lord, give her the living child, and in no wise slay it. But the other said, Let it be neither mine nor thine, but divide it. Then the King answered and said: Give her the living child and in no wise slay it: she is the mother thereof. And all Israel heard of the Judgement... and they feared the King, for they saw that the wisdom of God was in him.

And of course, the Book of Proverbs and the Song of Solomon were his greatest literary achievements; 'He spake three thousand proverbs and his songs were a thousand and five.' But as far as we are concerned, the building of the Holy Temple at Jerusalem was his lasting legacy. It is recorded in the Bible (I Kings 5:13) that:

King Solomon conscripted labourers from all Israel – 30,000 men. He sent them off to Lebanon in shifts of 10,000 a month, so that they spent one month in Lebanon and two months home. Solomon had 70.000 carriers and 80,000 stonecutters in the hills.

There were also 3,300 overseers who supervised the project and directed the workmen. At the King's command they removed from the quarry large blocks of quality stone to provide a foundation of dressed stone for the temple.

Of course, those readers who are familiar with the Mark Degree will appreciate the extra significance of the stonemasons' activities and the serious responsibility placed on the overseers to ensure that the quarried stones met strict standards, both of quality and dimension. According to 1 Kings 5:17:

...and the King commanded, and they brought great stones, costly stones and hewed stones, to lay the foundations of the house. And Solomon's builders and Hiram's builders did hew them, and the stone-squarers: so they prepared timber and stones to build the house.

Shortly after, in I Kings 6:7: we learn that:

...the house, when it was in building, was built of stone made ready before it was brought hither: so that there was neither hammer nor axe, nor any tool of iron heard in the house, while it was in building.

We must of course remember at this point, where those skilled workmen went to receive their wages. According to 1 Kings 6 v.8:

The door for the middle chamber was in the right side of the house: and they went up with winding stairs into the middle chamber and out of the middle chamber into the third. They of course received them without scruple or diffidence: ...without scruple, knowing they were justly entitled to them, and without diffidence from the great reliance they placed on the integrity of their employers in those days.

We come finally to the two great pillars, which stood at the porch way or entrance of King Solomon's Temple. Unfortunately, the Bible offers no evidence that they were named after any particular persons, in fact all the evidence suggests that they were derived from the Hebrew words 'in strength' and 'to establish' It is probably a coincidence that the one on the left was named *Boaz*, which happens to be the same name as the husband of Ruth, whereas the name *Jachin* appears nowhere else in the Holy Scriptures. In the explanation of the Second Degree Tracing Board, we are informed that:

...the height of these pillars was seventeen and a half cubits each, their circumference twelve, their diameter four; they were formed hollow, the better to serve as archives to Freemasonry, for therein were deposited the constitutional rolls. Being formed hollow, their outer rim or shell was four inches or a hand's breadth in thickness. They were made of molten Brass, and were cast in the clay ground on the banks of the Jordan, between Succoth and Zeradatha.

Ironically, both Kings and Chronicles provide us with an identical account of their manufacture;

'In the plain of Jordan did the King cast them, in the clay ground between Succoth and Zeradatha.'

Sadly however, nowhere does the Bible contain any mention that they were formed hollow so as to serve as archives to Freemasonry. Nevertheless, the erection of those two famous pillars is well documented again in both Kings and Chronicles, the most detailed of which may be found in 1 Kings 7:15-21:

> For he cast two pillars of brass, of eighteen cubits high apiece: and a line of twelve cubits did compass either of them about. And he made two chapiters of molten brass, to set upon the tops of the pillars: the height of the one chapiter was five cubits and the height of the other chapiter was five cubits: and nets of checkerwork, and wreaths of chain work for the chapiters which were on the top of the pillars: seven for the one chapiter and seven for the other chapiter. There were two rows of pomegranates, four cubits of lilywork and two hundred pomegranates in rows. And he set up the pillars in the porch of the temple: and he set up the right pillar, and called the name thereof Jachin; and he set up the left of the pillars and called the name thereof Boaz.

There are some of course, who may not have noticed that despite the order of erection just mentioned, the candidate's attention is directed only to the left hand pillar during his initiation, while the right hand pillar is kept for his passing. There are several other paradoxes, particularly the absence of any mention whatsoever in the Bible, of the death of our Master, Hiram Abif. The building of the first temple at Jerusalem was indeed his greatest masterpiece. Its significance is central to Freemasonry, particularly, the two pillars, the winding staircase and general layout. Were it not for Solomon's magnificent achievement and reputation, it is doubtful whether Zerubbabel's replacement Temple would ever have been built some five hundred years later. Without such an event, it is probable that our glorious Royal Arch Degree would never have existed.

It is recorded that in the fifth year of the reign of Rehoboam, soon after the death of Solomon, Shishak, the King of Egypt pillaged the temple and as it says in *Kings*:

> ...and he took away the treasures of the house of the Lord and the treasures of the King's house - and he took away all the shields of gold which Solomon had made - and King Rehoboam made in their stead brazen shields.

Then in the reign of Josiah the temple structure needed to be repaired. The Book of Chronicles states:

> And at the King's commandment they made a chest and set it without at the gate of the house of the Lord - And all the princes and all the people rejoiced and brought in and cast into the chest.
>
> Now it came to pass that at that time the chest was brought unto the King's office by the hands of the Levites, and when they saw that there was

much money, the King's scribe and the High Priest's officer came and emptied the chest. This they did day-by-day and gathered money in abundance.

Eventually, in the reign of King Darius, it is recorded in Haggai, 1:14 that Zerubbabel was inspired to rebuild the temple, with the alleged discovery of the underground chamber, so vital to Royal Arch ceremonies:

> Then Haggai, the Lord's messenger, gave this message of the Lord to the people: 'I am with you,' declares the Lord. So the Lord stirred up the spirit of Zerubbabel son of Shealtiel, governor of Judah, and the spirit of Joshua son of Jehozadak, the high priest, and the spirit of the whole remnant of the people. They came and began to work on the house of the Lord Almighty, their God, on the twenty-fourth day of the sixth month of the second year of King Darius.

We have taken a brief look at the significance of the Bible in Freemasonry, both from a symbolic and literary viewpoint. Perhaps its ultimate importance can best be expressed in the Craft Address to the newly installed Master:

> By a strict adherence to the By-laws of your Lodge, the Book of Constitutions, but above all, the Volume of the Sacred law, that Great Light, which is given as a rule and guide to our faith, you will be enabled to lay up a crown of joy and rejoicing, which will never fade, but will remain until time shall be no more, and may the Great Architect of the Universe give you health, strength and wisdom to conduct the affairs of your Lodge with credit to yourself and to the satisfaction of its members.

Let us never forget then, that although Freemasonry cannot be classified as a *religion*, the numerous specific Biblical references in our ritual may hopefully encourage us to make a greater study of the Sacred Volume and the invaluable precepts it contains.

CHAPTER SEVEN

FREEMASONRY UNDER ADVERSITY

IT HAS BEEN particularly rewarding to notice the way in which Freemasonry has so frequently triumphed over adversity, especially in the field of human conflict. Unfortunately there is not enough time to include for instance the privations of Freemasons as a result of the *Papal Bull* issued by Pope Pius IX in 1738 against Freemasonry, threatening every member of the Brotherhood with excommunication. Instead this paper concentrates specifically on the theatres of War – including the Boer War, the Wars in Europe and also in the Pacific. But let us begin with the American War of Independence:

In North America back in the1770s, English Freemasons found themselves pitted against their American Brothers but sometimes on the battlefield, when death stared them in the face, the friendly hand of a Mason was often outstretched to save those, who by word or sign, could show that they shared a similar obligation to care for each other's wants and afflictions.

At the Battle of Stony Point in Pennsylvania on July 16th 1779, the British 17th Regiment of Foot was captured, and being a Military Lodge, its warrant and regalia were brought to the Attention of General Samuel Parsons, a Member of the American Union Lodge, Connecticut. He immediately ordered that the seized Masonic material be sent straight back to the enemy Brethren, with the following letter:

> Brethren: When the ambition of monarchs or jarring interest of contending states, call forth their subjects to war, as Masons, we are disarmed of that resentment, which stimulates to undistinguished desolation; and however our political sentiments may impel us in the public dispute, we are still Brethren, and our professional duty apart, ought to promote the happiness and advance the wellbeing of each other. Accept therefore, at the hands of a Brother, the Documents, which your late misfortunes have put in my power to restore to you. I am your Brother and obedient servant, Samuel H. Parsons.

The next major conflict in the United States was from 1861-1865, between the Confederates and the Unionists. (Incidentally, I might add here that Freemasonry was very well established in the United Kingdom at that time, under the supervision of the Right Worshipful Grand Master, the Earl of Zetland.) One of the first acts of Masonic Charity to occur in the American Civil War occurred at the First Battle of Manassas on July 21st, 1861.

Colonel W.H. Raynor of the Unionist 1st Ohio Regiment left his command and in the company of two sergeants went to fetch water at a nearby creek. Suddenly, as they neared the stream, they heard the yell that eventually became known as the 'rebel yell' and the thundering hooves of hundreds of horses. One of them fired his pistol at Raynor and missed but as he passed by struck Raynor with his sabre. Lights flashed through Raynor's brain and he fell to the ground senseless appearing almost dead.

Later coming completely to his senses, Raynor realised he was surrounded by the Confederate cavalry. Two cavalrymen seeing him staggering there grabbed him between their horses and dragged him off a considerable distance. Finally one lifted him and placed him in front of him on his horse. They rode till they came to a group of Rebel wounded. Raynor was taken first to a surgeon who refused to treat him because he was a Yankee and who said that he had enough others to take care of from his own army.

Finally another more compassionate surgeon was found and his wounds were taken care of. He was made as comfortable as possible. His guard, J.H. Lemon of Radford's Cavalry truly acted the part of the Good Samaritan. Lemon somewhere found some ice and put it on the pounding head of Raynor and inquired if Raynor needed any money.

In response to Raynor's expressions of gratitude, pointing to the Masonic pin on Raynor's shirt, Lemon replied, 'I can only hope to get the same treatment from your men if I ever fall into their hands. If you will relieve the distresses of a suffering Brother Mason when in your power, I shall be well paid.' Lemon then mounted his horse and rode away. There were predictably many similar acts of Brotherhood during four years of bloody conflict.

Back in Europe in major armed conflicts such as the Peninsular and Napoleonic Wars, great numbers of prisoners captured on both sides would include large numbers of Freemasons. Apparently, both Wellington and Napoleon were 'On the square', the former having been initiated into Lodge No. 494, while a Colonel in the 33rd Regiment of Foot, and the latter in 1798 at a Lodge in Valetta, Malta.

There is ample evidence that in both England and France, members of the Craft readily came to the assistance of their poor and distressed brethren, and that when, as was the case with the French Prisoners in this country, they formed Lodges of their own, the members visited and were visited by the local Lodge, or even the Lodges in towns that they happened to be passing through while marching from one prison to another.

The conditions under which the French prisoners of war lived varied very much. In the 1850s and 60s their number was not great, but even then we hear of 11,000 located near Bristol, suffering much for want of food and clothing. But in the Napoleonic wars, when over 122,000 were brought over, the prison accommodation was wholly inadequate, and the authorities put them where they could, being reduced to using the unserviceable ships lying in the harbours of Chatham, Plymouth and Portsmouth, where conditions were truly awful. Yet even here the prisoners opened their Lodges and worked in the most miserable surroundings. A hulk at Portsmouth, the *Guildford,* which was used as a prison, also had a Lodge, and a certain Bro. Lardier visited it. He later wrote the following account:

After traversing the whole length of the lowest deck we came to a trap-door; this was raised and we descended into the darkness down a short ladder and continued a few paces forward from its foot, led by the hand of our conductor. After giving the passwords, signs and grips, we were permitted to enter the Lodge. The chamber was illuminated only by a piece of candle inserted in the neck of an old beer-bottle which, set before the Master's Chair, made so much smoke that only a feeble, glimmering ray of light was visible.

The Master's Chair was a dilapidated bench with only three legs remaining, upon which he did his best to maintain equilibrium. He was the only one to have a seat. The rest of us, members of the Lodge and visitors alike, were requested to sit down upon the floor. The unsuitability of the place rendered much of the ritual impossible. But the candidate was rigorously interrogated about his principles and more especially about his patriotism. His replies were satisfactory and he was received into Freemasonry.

It is ironic that the forthcoming Boer war would see South African prisoners incarcerated on the same island as Napoleon: St Helena. Many of those prisoners were Freemasons, hailing from Lodges under the Grand Lodge of the Netherlands, and were grateful to receive copies of *Masonic Illustrated* from England and to be allowed parole to attend local Lodges. One such Brother wrote to that colourful Masonic publication:

> Existence here is very dull, and a few of us are indebted to the local Lodges for being enabled to spend a few pleasant evenings in the town at Lodge meetings. Whatever our political differences are, we have had no reason to complain of our fellow craftsmen, who have in a most generous way extended to many of us the right hand of fellowship and welcome. And when release does come, our recollections of Masonic ties in St. Helena will be carried from this island, and will have a better influence in healing the sore places than all the sophistry of statesmen and legislators.

Meanwhile between 25th November, and March 5th 1901, during the Siege of Ladysmith, members of the Biggarsberg Lodge of Unity and the Ladysmith Mark Masons Lodge held frequent meetings in spite of regular shelling by the Boer artillery, moving premises according to damage and danger. In fact all Lodge records were initially buried for safekeeping, but when it became obvious that the siege might become prolonged, they were retrieved and kept up to date, with entries such as:

> On the 29th November 1900, an emergency meeting of the Lodge was held at the Royal Hotel, a place that had been deserted by its former occupants, owing to the continual shelling, the Boers having concentrated their fire on

this place; and there, on the 31st day of the siege, was initiated into Masonry a gentleman, a townsman of Ladysmith, aged fifty-five, in the presence of some sixty to seventy brethren, all of whom were either wearing the Queen's uniform or the badge of the Town Guard.

The First World War soon followed, but with similar instances of Masonic forbearance being recorded: On Christmas Day in 1914, fighting stopped for 22 miles along the British lines in Flanders, Christmas trees appeared and at first a few cautious heads were raised above the parapets. Then, not having been fired at, others boldly stood up to wish the enemy a Happy Christmas and advanced across no-man's land to shake hands with their German counterparts.

The grip would instantly have identified a brother, and for the rest of the day badges, food, cigarettes and addresses were exchanged. A football match was also rumoured to have taken place. Unfortunately, the conflict was resumed the following day. The thought of Lodges attempting to hold meetings under persistent bombardment and in the awful trenches of the Somme defies our imagination.

The following examples appertain to more recent times. During the Second World War relationships between the two major protagonists were of such a nature as not to bring about any kind of truce, except total capitulation. Freemasonry apparently continued to function under adversity in no less than fourteen Prisoner of War camps throughout Germany, Austria and elsewhere in Europe. We are grateful for the unpublished accounts of Brother Selby-Boothroyd who was captured in May 1940 and in January 1944 he arrived at Oflag 8F in Mahrisch Trubau.

Some months after his arrival, he learned that some forty Brethren, transferred from an Italian camp, were holding meetings. Initially these comprised little more than opening and closing ceremonies. The Senior Chaplain of the camp was a member of the craft, and he allowed the Brethren to meet in the camp Chapel under the guise of attending theological lectures. It was a common practice at such gatherings for the Master or someone else to be ready to lecture on some pre-arranged subject at a moment's notice if an alarm was sounded.

In May 1944 the whole camp was moved to Oflag 79 at Brunswick. The Lodge was kept intact and soon became firmly established. In due time it included Brethren from England Scotland, Australia, Canada, New Zealand, India, South Africa and the United States. At first it met weekly in the air-raid shelters with which the camp was well supplied, it being a former Luftwaffe camp and airfield. The shelters made admirable Lodge rooms and were lit with electricity, but during air-raids the power was cut off so they were obliged to resort to 'margarine lamps'. These were manufactured by purifying margarine (when available) and pouring the liquid into a cut-down tin with a piece of string or an old pyjama cord as a wick.

The Second World War brought Masonry into many more areas of public conflict and private grief. On the Nazi occupation of the Channel Islands in 1940, the Masonic Temple at Jersey was sacked and its contents were removed on Hitler's orders for a major exhibition in Berlin, whose purpose was an attempt to prove that the links between Freemasonry and the Jewish Religion had the secret object of achieving World Domination.

Many German Freemasons were rounded up and sent to concentration camps, while others were determined to hold clandestine meetings and sometimes risked their lives to help British prisoners-of-war to escape. In fact soon after Hitler's rise to power in 1934, it became apparent that German Freemasonry was in danger. In the same year the German Grand Lodge of Bayreuth realised the very imminent problems facing them and suggested that Masons should wear a little blue flower, the *forget-me-not*, instead of the traditional square and compasses.

It was felt the new symbol would not attract the attention of Nazis, who were busy confiscating and appropriating Masonic Lodges and property. Masonry had gone underground and it was necessary to have some readily recognisable means of identification. Throughout the entire Nazi era, a little blue flower in a lapel secretly identified a Brother.

In the concentration camps and in the cities, a little blue forget-me-not distinguished the lapels of those who refused to allow the light of Masonry to be extinguished. Thus did a simple flower blossom forth into a meaningful emblem of the Fraternity and has become perhaps the most widely worn pin among Freemasons in Germany. In many British Lodges, the forget-me-not is still presented to newly raised Master Masons, at which time it is briefly explained.

British Freemasons were not the only Brethren to hold their German Brothers in such high regard. On a personal note, my wife and I were celebrating the arrival of the New Year in a restaurant not far from Dieppe in France, when I noticed a small pin in the lapel of a Frenchman who was sharing our table with his wife. 'What's that emblem on your jacket?' I enquired. 'Oh, just decoration!' was his casual reply. 'A bit like this?' I suggested, turning over my Masonic ring. 'Exactly like that!' he exclaimed. Thereafter, the conversation flowed freely and easily between us, and the evening concluded with my receiving three kisses, and three more from the male singer/conjuror who it turned out was a member of the same French Lodge.

What transpired in that long conversation was truly enlightening; the strong emotional feelings, which the French Masons still hold for their German Brothers from the time of the Nazi occupation. Apparently, although it is nowhere written down, those Freemasons, who now found themselves an occupying force, took tremendous personal risks to assist and protect their French Brothers, even to collaborating as much as they dared with the Resistance. The penalty they faced if detected, was that of torture and the firing squad, while their family would be rounded up and sent to the concentration camps. Nevertheless, they remained as true as they could be, to their Masonic obligation.

Towards the end of the War, our anger and indignation was focused on the inhumane treatment of Allied prisoners in Japanese Camps. The Japanese were not against Freemasonry as such, but against gatherings of any kind, which they always suspected of plotting something like mass escapes.

It was perhaps fitting that the last pre-surrender meeting on February 12th 1943 should have been held by one of the oldest Lodges in Singapore - Lodge Zetland in the East No. 508. Ventilation was adequate for two or three persons, but not for 20 Lodge members. There was neither Lodge furniture nor regalia. Voices were hushed. Outside the door stood a Tyler more vigilant than ever and supported by a string of Assistant Tyler's picketed at intervals along the corridors of the ground floor.

They were each in possession of a prearranged signal to warn of approaching Japanese. Meetings continued to be held in Changi Prison with fair regularity until the 10th October 1943.

After that date the Camp languished under a harsh and vigilant Gestapo supervision for many months. It was utterly impossible to risk holding further Masonic meetings. The situation was little better in Stanley Internment Camp, Hong Kong, and I would like to finish this paper with an extract from the outgoing Master of Cathay Lodge at its Installation meeting on March 5th 1943. For me, it encapsulates the spirit of Freemasonry to which we can all turn for inspiration and encouragement:

First of all I would like to thank all officers and Brethren for their splendid support whilst we were able to be together. Cathay Lodge had the honour of holding the last regular meeting in the district prior to commencement of hostilities, and I did say that it may be the last meeting we should have for some time and that if anything happened we should all endeavour to live up to our Masonic ideals. Like many more I have lost practically everything I possessed and there have been times in this camp when I have been almost down and out. I have then found some helping hands outstretched to me and I have been grateful and I think that has happened to most of us. However I feel that a little more fellowship and brotherly love would help us all considerably to carry on until we are once again free.

If my last speech at Zetland Hall was in any form of prophecy, then I sincerely hope that what I have to say now will react in a like manner. That is – that this war will soon be over, that we all be united with our loved ones and take up our Masonic career where we left off. When we get back into the outside world I would ask you to turn up for the first Lodge meeting that is convened. Do not let the loss of a dress suit or your regalia deter you. I am sure the District Grand Master will grant a dispensation to wear welfare shorts and a flour sack sewn with blue ribbon if necessary.

We have just taken a brief look at Freemasonry under adversity over a couple of centuries, and can now reflect on the strength of purpose and camaraderie, which only our unique Order appears to offer. Hopefully, in a world of continuing conflict and uncertainty, Freemasons around the world will eventually bring their convictions to bear upon those who would otherwise impose their selfish motives upon others. Let us therefore always go our separate ways in peace and with goodwill towards all mankind.

References:

A. E. Roberts, *House Undivided: The Story of Freemasonry and the Civil War*, Macoy Publishing & Masonic Supply Co, Richmond, VA 1976

M. M. Johnson, *The Beginnings of Freemasonry in America*, 1924

A. E. Roberts, *Freemasonry in American History*, Macoy Publishing & Masonic Supply Co, Richmond, VA 1985

R. Melzer, *In the Eye of a Hurricane: German Freemasonry in the Weimar Republic and the Third Reich*, *Heredom* Vol. 10, pp 203-221, Scottish Rite Journal of Freemasonry 2002

CHAPTER EIGHT

ENGLISH NOBILITY AND FREEMASONRY

King Edward VII
(*Gould's History of Freemasonry, 1886*)

ONE OF THE most active and influential English Grand Masters: King Edward the Seventh, his brother the Duke of Connaught and his son, the Duke of Clarence, both also Freemasons, epitomise the important place of the Nobility in Freemasonry ever since 1721, when English Grand Masters have been established members of the Nobility. According to the distinguished Oxford historian, John Roberts in 1969, they have similarly included seven Princes of the blood. Our overseas Grand Masters however, have also featured, in 1888, Oscar, King of Sweden; in 1891 The Crown Prince, later King Frederick of Denmark; in 1937, King Christian of Denmark, and also in 1947, King Gustaf of Sweden.

It is widely believed that without the patronage of the ruling classes in the late seventeenth and early eighteenth centuries, Freemasonry could not exist in its present form or even at all. Tempting though it is to dwell on a chronological study of our illustrious forebears, it is more important to recognise their invaluable contribution to the development of Freemasonry, as we know it today.

To begin with, let us remember, 'In a society so widely extended as Freemasonry, whose branches are spread over the four quarters of the globe, it cannot be denied that we have many members of rank and opulence.' We must also recall that 'Monarchs themselves have been promoters of the art, have not thought it derogatory to their dignity to exchange the sceptre for the trowel, have participated in our mysteries and have joined in our assemblies.'

In order to appreciate the special relationship between our 'Noble' Masonic Brothers and the ordinary members of the Craft, we need to consider at least one of the many theories surrounding the origins of Free and Accepted or Speculative Masonry. Let's begin with one of the simplest, at the construction of all stately and superb edifices such as manor houses and cathedrals; it would have first been customary in this country, for the builders to furnish themselves with accommodation, which may well have had to stand for many years. These 'Lodges' would provide a temporary home for the many operatives and their apprentices, who travelled long distances to offer their services.

It is quite understandable, as actual or perceived benefactors, those wealthy landowners and other potential patrons would be invited to attend operative Lodge meetings, as and when they became more formalised. Such meetings burgeoned in popularity, and as the number of Lodges increased over time some eventually lost all their operative stonemasons. It is possible that surviving members would continue to reinforce the value and meaning of their activities by employing the symbolic nature of stonemason's working tools as guidelines for moral and spiritual development, and by placing emphasis on the secrecy and uniqueness of the ceremonies.

Bernard Jones, in his *Guide and Compendium,* suggests that:

> ...the English accepted or adopted Mason of the seventeenth century was much more than, and essentially different from, a non-operative member. In the Mason Company there might be, on the one hand, operative masons and, on the other, men who may not have touched a tool in all their lives – 'gentlemen' who had come in by patrimony or gift of membership.

In his *History of Freemasonry* published in 1886, Robert Freke Gould prefers the theory that the term 'Freemason' was generally used to distinguish an operative Mason who was also a Freeman of the City of London, following the Great Fire of 1666, when the erection of wooden buildings were subsequently prohibited and a serious influx of foreigners were needed for the rebuilding of London and St Paul's

Cathedral. By a Statute of 1666, entitled *An Act for the rebuilding of the City of London* it was ordained:

> ...that all Carpenters, Bricklayers, Masons, Plaisterers, Joyners, and other Artificers, Workmen and Labourers, to be employed on the said Buildings [in the City of London], who are not Freemen of the said Citty, shall for the space of seaven yeares next ensueing, and for soe long time after as until the said buildings shall be fully finished, have and enjoy such and the same liberty or workeing and being sett to worke in the said building as the Freemen of the Citty of the same Trades and Professions have and ought to enjoy.

Even today, the Guild of Freemen Lodge No. 3525 offers membership specifically to liverymen and those who have been awarded the Freedom of the City of London. Robert Freke Gould further advocates that this Act, by diminishing the powers of the companies, paved the way for the development of English Freemasonry in its present form. By 1686 the term *'Freemason'* was readily in use, when Dr Robert Plot a Fellow of the Royal Society included the following account in his *Natural History of Staffordshire*:

> ...to these add the Customs relating to the County, wherof they have one, of admitting Men into the Society of Free-Masons, that in the moorelands of this County seems to be of greater request, than anywhere else, though I find the Custom spread more or less all over the Nation; for here I found persons of the most eminent quality, that did not disdain to be of this Fellowship.

Two years later marked the publication in 1688 of *Academie of Armory* by Randle Holme, a herald and deputy to the Garter King of Arms for Cheshire, Lancashire, Shropshire and North Wales. Referring to Freemasonry, he writes:

> ... a fraternity or Society or Brotherhood, or Company; are such in corporation, that are of one and the same trade, or occupation, who being joined together by oath and covenant, do follow such orders and rules, as are made, or to be made for the good order, rule and support of such and every of their occupations. I cannot but honour the Fellowship of the Masons because of its Antiquity; and the more, as being a Member of that Society, called Free-masons.

The next thirty years would see the emergence of Free, Accepted or Speculative Masonry and the development of Freemasons' Lodges throughout the country, much closer to their present form. This is explained by William Sandys, Fellow of the Antiquarian Society, Past Master of the Grand Masters, Lodge No.1, and author in 1829 of *A Short History of Freemasonry* he writes:

It appears that speculative Masonry, to which alone the term 'Free-masonry' is now applied, was scarcely known before the time of Sir Christopher Wren; that it was engrafted upon Operative Masonry, which at that time was frequently called Free-Masonry, adopting the signs and symbols of the operative Masons.

According to William Sandys:

> Elias Ashmole was made a Mason at Warrington in the year 1646. At the same time a Society of Rosicrucians had been formed in London... Among other emblems, they made use of the sun, moon, compasses, square, triangle etc. Ashmole and some of his literary friends belonged to this society, which met in Mason's Hall as well as (belonging to) to the Mason's Company, and they revised and added to the peculiar emblems and ceremonies of the latter which were simple, and had been handed down to them through many ages.

The above theory is further developed by Edward Waite in his *Encyclopaedia of Freemasonry*, where he postulates that the Grand Lodge of 1717:

> ...was formed of the remnants of a society in and about London, which had lost its raison d'être as a Trade Guild, which no longer consisted exclusively or even generally of persons belonging to the building Trade, but which continued to meet in various Lodges and to transact some kind of formal business, including the admission of fresh persons within their ranks. When the business was over, there followed a meal in common.

The principal impetus was supplied in Waite's view '...by the 'group of literati' who were gathered within the walls of Grand Lodge.' Four London Lodges were credited with the foundation of modern day Freemasonry in 1717, and met respectively at the Goose and Gridiron in St Paul's Churchyard, the Crown in Parker's Lane near Drury Lane, the Apple Tree in Charles Street, Covent Garden and the Rummer and Grapes in Channel Row, Westminster. By 1723 the first had twenty-two members, the second; twenty-one, the third; fourteen, including the first Grand Master: Anthony Sayer, and the fourth, seventy-one, which included '...ten noblemen, three honourables, four baronets or knights, seven colonels, two clergymen and twenty-four esquires'.

The latter Lodge also boasted as members, Doctor James Anderson, George Payne, the Antiquary and second Grand Master; and Doctor John Desaguliers who became the third Grand Master in 1719. Those first three Grand Masters were the *only* rulers of the Craft not to have been Nobly or Royally born, thereafter the list of Grand Masters is liberally sprinkled with Lords, Marquesses, Viscounts, Earls, Dukes, and Princes. The lower orders of Masonic hierarchy feature countless Knights, landed gentry, doctors of divinity, and other men of letters, whose main contribution to Freemasonry was in the written word. Chief among them were the barrister, Robert Freke Gould, the theologian, Doctor George Oliver, the journalist, William Preston and Doctor of Divinity, James Anderson, author of our current *Constitutions*.

The need for a 'Noble Brother' at the helm of the Society was satisfied in 1721 by the installation of John, 2nd Duke of Montague. On that very same occasion, according to Doctor James Anderson in his *Constitutions*, 'Philip, Lord Stanhope – afterwards Earl of Chester was made a Mason' and during 1722, Doctor Anderson goes on to observe that many noblemen and gentlemen of the first rank:

> …desired to be admitted into the fraternity, besides other learned men… It has been said in view of these facts, but more especially on the accession of Montague, that the Masonic Society rose at one bound into notice and esteem.

By 1725 the number of Lodges under the umbrella of the Grand Lodge of England had risen to sixty-four and some clear way of indicating a Grand Lodge Officer's rank seemed necessary. By 1731 the Grand Master; Thomas Coke, Lord Lovell had approved regulations determining the Regalia to be worn by his Officers. In 1737, Frederick, the Prince of Wales was initiated into the Craft. Quite apart from the gravitas and respectability, which members of the nobility brought to Freemasonry, their organisational skills and obvious authority ensured that every detail of our assemblies was meticulously planned and executed. The only sad exception was recorded however, in the case of Lord Byron, who became Grand Master in 1747 and apart from attending his installation and proposing Lord Carysfort as his successor, spent the whole time abroad. Lord Carysfort was installed as Grand Master in 1752. Ironically, the next year, in response to complaints of certain 'irregularities' among members, it was enacted:

> …that no Lodge shall ever make a Mason without due inquiry into his character, neither shall any Lodge be permitted to make and raise the same Brother at one and the same Meeting, without a dispensation from the Grand Master, which on very particular occasions may be requested.

In 1767, the Duke of Beaufort was elected Grand Master, and one of his important decisions was that Grand Lodge ought to have appropriate premises from which to administer the growing number of Lodges around the country. He also believed that the Society's legal status should be formally registered. In October 1769 it was proposed:

> …that to have the Society incorporated and proposed that the Brethren present should take into serious consideration the most effectual means to raise a fund for defraying the expense of building a hall.

It was subsequently agreed that certain fees should be paid: by the Grand Officers annually, by new Lodges at their constitution, by Brethren at initiation or joining and for dispensations. By 1773, it was required that each Lodge would:

> ...transmit to the Grand Secretary, a list of its members, with the dates of their admission or initiation; also their ages, together with their titles, professions, or trades; and that five shillings be transmitted for every initiate, and half-a-crown for each joining member.

Premises for the new hall were obtained in 1774 at a cost of £3150 in Great Queen Street. The foundation stone was laid on May 1st 1775 and the Society's new premises were opened a year later and dedicated '…in solemn form to Masonry, Virtue, Universal Charity and Benevolence.' The dedication necessitated the creation of two new offices, that of Grand Architect, which was filled by the building's designer, Thomas Sandby, and also that of Grand Chaplain, the first incumbent being the Reverend William Dodd, Doctor of Laws. Unfortunately, Doctor Dodd was convicted of fraud the following April and thrown into Newgate Prison. He was quite understandably expelled from the Society.

The authorising of new Lodges, issuing Warrants, dealing with petitions, revising the Book of Constitutions, settling disputes, making regulations; these were all grist to the mill for our Grand Masters. To add to their challenges, a rival Grand Lodge had been formed in 1751 by some independently minded Freemasons who believed that they practiced a pure and ancient form of Masonry and accordingly called themselves the *Antients*. They therefore regarded the established Grand Lodge as the *Moderns*.

The Antients were generally composed of the social underclass, shopkeepers, mechanics, and those in similar occupations, although they were presided over by many influential Masons, including the Earl of Bleniston, the Earl of Antrim, and the third and fourth Dukes of Atholl. In 1813 a compromise was reached and Masonry became once more united thanks to the determination of Augustus Frederick, Duke of Sussex who succeeded the Prince of Wales for the *Moderns* and the Duke of Kent for the Antients.

The symbolic meeting, called the 'Lodge of Reconciliation' was held on St. John's Day, December 27th 1813, with representatives of the Antients and Moderns arranged on the two sides of Freemason's Hall in such a way as they were completely intermingled. The two Grand Masters were seated on either side of the Chair of King Solomon. The Act of Union was then read out and was accepted, ratified and confirmed by the Brethren assembled. *One* Grand Lodge was then constituted and the Duke of Kent as Grand Master of the Ancient Fraternity proposed His Royal Highness, the Duke of Sussex to be the Grand Master of the United Grand Lodge of Ancient Freemasons for the ensuing year. This was put to the vote and the Duke of Sussex duly took his seat.

Having welcomed the Prince of Wales into the Craft, at the following meeting of Grand Lodge, it was announced that the year before, Prince William Henry (later to become King William IV) had already been initiated into Prince George Lodge, Plymouth, and it was agreed to present him with an apron lined with blue silk, with the invitation to attend future meetings as a Past Grand Master. Of course, the Prince of Wales already owned a similar apron, adorned with the 'Prince of Wales' feathers and which may still be viewed today at the Sussex Masonic Centre, not far from the Royal Pavilion for which he was famous or rather infamous, to the point where Queen Victoria refused ever to visit it on account of its reputation as a '…whore-house built for the Prince's pleasure'.

Prince of Wales Apron
(*Author's photograph – courtesy of Reg Barrow, Curator, Provincial Grand Lodge of Sussex*)

The same presentation and privileges were subsequently offered to other sons of King George III: when they entered the Fraternity: The Duke of York in 1787; Prince Edward, later the Duke of Kent sometime around 1790; Prince Ernest, later the Duke of Cumberland, in 1796 and Prince Augustus, later Duke of Sussex in 1798. The King's son-in-law, Prince William, later Duke of Gloucester was also initiated into the Craft in 1795.

In 1790, Lord Rawdon, soon to become the Earl of Moira, was appointed Acting Grand Master, a position that he retained when the Prince of Wales became Grand Master in the November of that year. It was the Earl of Moira and the Duke of Atholl, who by giving assurances to the Prime Minister; William Pitt, managed to exempt Freemasonry from an Act of Parliament which was passed,'…for the more effectual suppression of Societies established for seditious and treasonable purposes'.

It was enacted that: …all societies, the members whereof are required to take any oath not authorised by law, shall be deemed unlawful combinations and confederacies' but it then went on expressly to state that, '…all societies holden under the Denomination of Loges of Freemasons, in conformity to the Rules prevailing in such Societies of Freemasons are exempted from the operation of the act.'

Robert Gould reinforces the importance of the Royal Connection, when he says:

> The Freemasons owe a deep debt of gratitude to the Royal Family of this country. Their immunity from the 'Secret Societies Act' of 1799 was due in great measure to the circumstances of the heir to the throne being at the Head of the Older Society.

Thirty years later, in 1828, a special Grand Lodge was held at the Thatched House Tavern, St. James Street. Its purpose was to install the Duke of Clarence, Lord High Admiral, as Master of the Prince of Wales' Lodge, because the Grand Master, the Duke of Sussex was convinced '…that it was of the first importance to obtain the Sanction and Protection of the Royal Family to the Proceedings of the Craft.' When King George IV died two years later, he was succeeded by King William IV as Patron of the Craft. Freemasonry has continued to enjoy the privilege of Royal Patronage ever since.

Before continuing with the *added value* of our more 'Noble' forebears, it must now be apparent that without them, Freemasonry would probably not exist at all, especially in view of the Act of Parliament just mentioned. A debt is therefore owed to those who worked hard to refine our Masonic laws and rituals, and ensured that records of our meetings and constitutions were diligently preserved.

Members of the English nobility obviously enjoyed their Masonry, and were keen to pass on those fraternal benefits to younger, aspiring men of rank and fortune. We the ordinary members also feel privileged to count noblemen among our Brothers. As we are reminded at each installation, 'Brethren, such is the nature of our Constitution that some must of necessity rule and teach; others of course must learn, submit and obey; humility in each being an essential virtue.'

It is with this humility that we salute our Grand Officers, but should we meet them at the Festive Board however, when the external trappings of rank have been put away, the warmth of their handshake will remind us that our 'Chiefs' also need committed 'Indians'. We are honoured that they choose to sojourn amongst us, while at the same time remembering that:

> …our Order should create within our hearts the amiable sentiments of honour, truth and virtue; it should lead us to shed a tear of sympathy o'er the failings of a brother and to pour the healing balm of consolation into the wounds of the afflicted.

In 1869, HRH, the Prince of Wales, later King Edward VII, became a member of the fraternity. At the Quarterly Communications of September 1869 the Earl of Zetland was proud to invest the Prince with the rank of 'Past Grand Master'. On the same evening he announced his intention to decline any future nomination for the office. His Royal Highness was subsequently installed as Grand Master at the Royal Albert Hall in London on 28th April 1875. On the Death of Queen Victoria in 1901, the Prince of Wales was crowned King and became protector of the Order. On the 17th July that year, the Duke of Connaught and Strathern was installed as Grand Master at the Royal Albert Hall.

One of the last significant contributions to the current state of Freemasonry by members of the English nobility occurred at the end of the First World War; On June 27th 1919 a special Grand Lodge was held at the Royal Albert Hall to celebrate the Peace. The Grand Master, the Duke of Connaught thereafter appealed to all Lodges of the English Constitution to assist in creating a new Grand Temple on the present site in Great Queen Street. This would form a Peace Memorial and a much larger home for Grand Lodge in perpetuity, the anticipated cost being a million pounds. A memorial fund was launched and Lodges were invited to contribute ten guineas per member to qualify as Hall-Stone Lodges. The building was fourteen years in construction and was inaugurated on July 19th 1933.

All in all, the English nobility may have had plenty of reasons for devoting so much of their time, money and energy in pursuit of their own Masonic interests, but along the way they have bequeathed the humblest members of our Society with a unique Brotherhood which cuts across social, racial and religious boundaries, to unite its members worldwide, in the furtherance of Brotherly harmony. Where else can such a fraternity be found?

I began by examining various theories surrounding the birth of Freemasonry, and the contribution of the nobility, who were keen to give it their patronage. I have also mentioned some of the key participants in the development of our familiar 'Landmarks'. I have also remarked upon the universal respect they gained for our Order and the benefits of their managerial and organisational abilities, and of course, their financial investment must not be overlooked at this point, particularly in the setting up of charities, which are still the envy of the world.

When we say we are Freemasons therefore, let us remember who helped safeguard our freedom of association with those of similar morals and persuasions. When we then add that we are proud of our noble antecedents and privileged to have enjoyed their patronage, let us lift our heads at the festive board perhaps just a little higher and address them in retrospect with the words, 'We greet you well!'

References:

R. Plot, *Natural History of Staffordshire*, University of Michigan, USA 1686

R. Holme, *Academie of Armory*, University of Michigan, USA 1688

E. Ashmole, *Antiquities of Berkshire*, University of Michigan, USA 1719

Dr J. Anderson, *Constitutions*, 1738 & 1756, Bernard Quaritch Ltd, London 1923

W. Sandys, *A Short History of Freemasonry*, Crew and Spencer, London 1829

R.F. Gould, *History of Freemasonry*, Thomas Jack, London 1886

E. Waite, *New Encyclopaedia of Freemasonry*, Rider & Co. London 1918

B. Jones, *Freemason's Guide and Compendium*, George Harrap, London 1950

Masonic Year Book, Historical Supplement, Grand Lodge of England, London 1964

CHAPTER NINE

NOT JUST GEOMETRY

Second Degree Tracing Board
(*Copyright HAL Harland/Lodge
of Economy No.7218*)

THE SECOND DEGREE Tracing Board has been widely regarded as the most instructive lecture for those Fellow Crafts lucky enough to enjoy it after their passing. Once the significance of the twin pillars and winding staircase has been explained, the exciting story of Jephtha and the Gileadites unfolds, followed by the numerical significance of the three Grand Masters, the five noble orders of architecture and the seven familiar arts and sciences. Fifty years ago, this would have been only a fraction of the detail explained in the *Emulation Ritual*, which had been firmly established from about 1870. We must of course bear in mind that the *Charge after Passing* reminds the Fellow Craft that:

> …the study of the liberal arts, which tends so effectually to polish and adorn the mind, is earnestly recommended to your consideration, especially the science of Geometry, which is established as the basis of our Art.

Bearing in mind that in the Second Degree ceremonies, we also invoke the blessing of the *Grand Geometrician of the Universe,* the Second Emulation Lecture informs us that Geometry was founded in the ancient Library of Alexandria in Egypt, which before it burnt down was the largest, and probably the most famous of the ancient world. It was a major centre of scholarship until many centuries after the Roman conquest of Egypt and for many centuries thereafter.

The reason given was that the River Nile, annually overflowing its banks, caused the inhabitants to retire to the high and mountainous parts of the country. When the waters subsided, they returned to their former habitations; but the floods frequently washing away their landmarks, caused grievous disputes among them, which often terminated in civil war. Apparently, it was once believed by some that on hearing of a Freemason's Lodge being held at Alexandria, the capital of their country, where Euclid presided, a deputation of the inhabitants repaired thither, and laid their grievances before him.

He, with the assistance of his Wardens and the rest of the Brethren, gathered together the scattered elements of Geometry, digested, arranged and brought them into a regular system, such as was practiced by most nations in those days, but is bettered in the present by the use of fluxions, conic sections and other improvements. By the science of Geometry, he taught the Egyptians to measure and ascertain the different districts of land and by that means put an end to their differences.

At this point it must be pointed out that the establishment of Emulation ritual was greatly influenced by Peter Gilkes from 1825 until his death in 1833. At that time a great deal of conjecture surrounded the origins of Freemasonry. The likelihood of it being already established in Egypt and the Greek mathematician Euclid even being a Worshipful Master is mere fanciful speculation. However, back in 1972 according to the Second Emulation Lecture, a Fellow Craft would probably have been overawed by its focus on the moral advantages especially when applied to Geometry.

As the Second Emulation Lecture explains, it is the first and noblest of sciences and is the basis on which the superstructure of Masonry is erected. By Geometry we may curiously trace nature through her various windings, to her most concealed recesses. By it we may discover the power, the wisdom and goodness of the Grand Geometrician of the Universe, and view with amazing delight the beautiful proportions, which connect and grace this vast machine. Also, by Geometry we may discover how the planets move in their different orbits, and mathematically demonstrate their various revolutions.

We may thereby rationally account for the return of seasons and the mixed variety of scenes, which each season produces to the discerning eye. Numberless worlds are around us, all formed by the same Divine artist, which roll through the vast expanse, and are conducted by the same unerring law of nature. While such objects engage our attention, how must we improve, and with what grand ideas must such knowledge fill our minds? It was a survey of nature and observation of her beautiful proportions, which first induced men to imitate the Divine plan, and study symmetry and order. This gave rise to society, and birth to every useful art. The architect began to design; and the plans, which he laid down, having been improved by time and experience, have produced some of those excellent works, which have been the admiration of every age.

According to the Emulation Lecture, the mystical number seven originated with the creation of Heaven and Earth by the Almighty, and all things therein and thereon contained in six days, and who rested on the seventh. The six periods of the creation are more elaborately described as follows, sadly without any valid scriptural references.

When we consider that the formation of the world was the work of the Omnipotent being who created this beautiful system of the universe, and caused all nature to be under His immediate care and protection:

How ought we to magnify and adore His Holy name, for His infinite wisdom, goodness and mercy to the children of men! Before it pleased the Almighty to command this vast whole into existence, the elements and materials of Creation lay blended together without form or distinction. Darkness was over the great deep, when the Spirit of God moved on the face of the waters. And as an example for man, that things of moment ought to be done with due deliberation, he was pleased to spend six days in commanding it from chaos to perfection.

The first instance of his supreme power was manifested by commanding *Light*. Being pleased with the operation of his Divine goodness, He gave it His sacred approbation, and distinguished it by a name; the light He called *Day*, and the darkness He called *Night*. In order to keep this new-framed matter within just limits, He spent the second period laying the foundation of the Heavens; which He called the *Firmament* and which was designed to keep the waters within the clouds and those beneath them fragmented.

The third period was employed in commanding the waters below into Due bounds; on the retreat of which, dry land appeared, which He called *Earth*, and the gathering together of the mighty waters, he called *Seas*. The earth being as yet irregular and uncultivated, God spoke the word, and it was immediately covered with a beautiful carpet of grass, designed as pasture for the initial creation; to which succeeded herbs, plants, flowers, shrubs and trees of all sorts, to full growth, maturity, and perfection.

On the fourth period, those two grand luminaries, the *Sun* and *Moon* were created; one to rule the day, and the other to govern the night. The sacred historian further informs us they were ordained for signs, and for seasons, for days and for years. Besides the Sun and Moon, the Almighty was pleased to bespangle the ethereal concave with a multitude of *Stars*; that man, whom He intended to make, might contemplate thereon, and justly admire the majesty and glory of his Creator.

On the fifth period, He created the birds to fly in the air, that man might please both his eyes and ears; by being delighted with some for their beautiful plumage and uncommon instincts, and with others for their melodious notes. He also in the same period caused the waters to bring forth a variety of fish; and to impress man with a reverential awe of His divine omnipotence, He created great whales; which with other inhabitants of the deep, after their kind, multiplied and increased exceedingly.

On the sixth period, He created the beasts of the field and the reptiles that crawl on the earth, and here we may plainly perceive the wisdom and goodness of the Almighty, made manifest in all His proceedings, by producing what effects he pleased without the aid of natural causes; such as giving light to the world before he created the Sun, and causing the earth to become fruitful without the influence of Heavenly Bodies.

He did not create the beasts of the field until he had provided for them with sufficient herbage for their support; nor did He make man until He had completed the rest of His works and finished and furnished him a dwelling, with everything requisite for life and pleasure. Then still more to dignify the work of His hands, He created man; who came into the world with greater splendour than any creature which had preceded Him; they coming into existence by no other than a single command, God spoke the word, and it was done, but at the formation of man there was a consultation.

God expressly said, let us make man, who was accordingly formed out of the dust of the earth, the breath of life was breathed into His nostrils, and man became a living soul. In this one creature was amassed whatever is excellent in the whole creation, the quality or substance of an animal being, the life of plants, the sense of beasts, and above all, the understanding of the Angels, created after the immediate image of God, with the rectitude of body; imitating thereby that integrity, and uprightness should ever influence Him to adore his Benign Creator, who had so liberally bestowed on Him the faculty of speech, and endued Him with that noble instinct called reason.

The Almighty, as His last, best gift to man, then created woman; under His forming hands a creature grew, man-like, but of different sex, so lovely and fair, that what seemed fair in all the world, now seemed mean, or in her summed up, in her contained. On she came, led by her heavenly master, though unseen, and guided by His voice; adorned with what all earth or heaven could bestow to make her amiable; grace was in her steps, heaven in her eye, in every gesture dignity and love.

After the sixth period, God's works being ended, He rested from His labour; He subsequently sanctified, blessed and hallowed the seventh day; thereby teaching men a useful lesson; to work six days industriously in support of themselves and their families, strictly commanding them to rest on the seventh, the better to contemplate on the works of the creation, and adore Him as their Creator; to go into His sanctuary to return thanks for their preservation, wellbeing, and all the other blessings they have so liberally received at His hands.

Having placed mankind on this earth according to Emulation studies, the Creator's next preoccupation appeared to be the evolution of architecture, on the basis that there is nothing more remarkable than Masonry and civilisation, like twin sisters, they have gone hand in hand. The orders of Architecture mark their growth and progress. Dark, dreary and comfortless were those days when Masonry had not laid her line nor extended her compass. The race of mankind, in full possession of wild and savage liberty, mutually afraid of, and offending each other, hid themselves in thickets of the wood, or in dens and caverns of the earth.

In those poor recesses and gloomy solitudes, Masonry found them, and the Grand Geometrician of the Universe, pitying their forlorn situation, instructed them to build houses for their ease, defence and comfort. It is easy to conceive that in the early state of society, genius had expanded but little. The first efforts were small, and the structure simple and rude, no more than a number of trees leaning together at the top, in the form of a cone, interwoven with twigs and plastered with mud to exclude the air and complete the work.

In this early period we may suppose each desirous to render his own habitation more convenient than his neighbour's, by improving on what had already been done. Thus, time, observation, assisting that natural sagacity inherent even in uncultivated minds, led them to consider the inconveniences of the round sort of habitation, and to build others, more spacious and convenient, of the square form, by placing trunks of trees perpendicularly in the ground to form the sides, filling the interstices between them with the branches, closely woven, and covered with clay. Horizontal beams were then placed on the upright trunks, which being strongly joined at the angles, kept the sides firm, and likewise served to support the covering or roof of the building, composed of joists on which were laid several beds of reeds, leaves and clay.

Yet, rough and inelegant as these buildings were, they had this salutary effect that, by aggregating mankind together they led the way to new improvements in arts and civilisation; for the hardest bodies will polish by collision, the roughest manners by communion and intercourse. Thus by degrees, mankind improved in the art of building, and invented methods to make their huts more lasting and handsome, as well as convenient. They took off the bark and other unevenness from the trunks of trees that formed the sides, raised them above the earth and humidity, on stones and covered each of them with a flat stone or tile to keep off the rain. The spaces between the ends of the joists they closed with clay or some other substance and the ends of the joists they covered with boards, cut in the manner of triglyphs. The form of the roof was likewise altered for, being, on account of its flatness, unfit to throw off the rain that fell in abundance during the winter seasons, they raised it in the middle, giving it the form of gable roof by placing rafters on the joists to support the clay, and other materials, that composed the covering.

From these simple forms the Orders of Architecture took their rise; for when the buildings of wood were set aside, and men began to erect solid and stately edifices of stone, they imitated the parts necessity had introduced into the primitive huts and adapted them in their temples which, although at first simple and rude, were in course of time, and by the ingenuity of succeeding architects, wrought and improved to such a degree of perfection on different models, that each was by way of eminence denominated an *Order*.

Of the orders, three are of the Grecian origin and are called Grecian orders. They are distinguished by the names of the Doric, Ionic and Corinthian; and exhibit three distinct characters of composition suggested by the diversity of form in the human frame. The other two are Roman orders; they are distinguished by the names of the Tuscan and Composite.

The Tuscan order is the simplest and most solid and is placed first in the list of the five Orders of Architecture on account of its plainness. Its column is seven diameters high, the base, capital, and entablature have but few moldings, and no other ornaments. Whence it has been compared to a sturdy laborer dressed in homely apparel. This order is no other that the Doric, more simplified, or deprived of its ornaments to suit certain purposes and adapted by the inhabitants of Tuscany, who were a colony of Dorian's. Yet there is a beauty in its simplicity, which adds to its value, and renders it fit to be used in structures where the rich and more delicate orders might be deemed superfluous.

The Doric is the first of the Grecian orders and is placed second in the list of the five Orders of Architecture. Its column, agreeable to modern proportions, is eight diameters high. It has no ornament except mouldings on either base or capital. Its frieze is distinguished by triglyphs (three bars) and *metopes*, (plain or carved mythological scenes) and its cornice above by *mutules*, representing the piece of timber through which the wooden pegs were driven in order to hold a rafter in position. Being the most ancient of all the orders, it retains more of the primitive hut style in its form than any of the rest. The triglyphs in the frieze represent the ends of the joists, and the mutules in its cornice represent the rafters.

The composition of this order is both grand and noble, being formed after the model of a muscular, full-grown man, delicate ornaments are repugnant to its characteristic solidity. It therefore succeeds best in the regularity of its proportions and is principally used in warlike structures where strength and a noble simplicity are required. At this era, their buildings, although admirably calculated for strength and convenience, wanted something in grace and elegance, which a continual observation of the softer sex supplied, for the eye that is charmed with symmetry must be conscious of woman's elegance and beauty.

This gave rise to the Ionic order. Its column is nine diameters high, its capital adorned with spiral volutes, and its cornice has dentils. History informs us that the famous Temple of Diana, at Ephesus, which was upwards of two hundred years in building, was composed of this order. Both elegance and ingenuity were displayed in the invention of this column. It is formed after the model of a beautiful young woman, of an elegant shape, dressed in her hair, as a contrast to that of the Doric, which represents a strong robust man.

Thus the human genius began to bud, the leaf and flower opening to perfection, producing the fairest and finest fruits, every liberal art, and every ingenious science, which could civilise, refine and exalt mankind. Then it was that Masonry put on her richest robes and decked herself in her most gorgeous apparel.

A new capital was invented at Corinth by the architect and sculptor Callimachus, which gave rise to the Corinthian, which is deemed the richest of the orders, and masterpiece of art. Its column is ten diameters high; its capital is adorned with two rows of leaves, and eight volutes, which sustain the abacus. This order is chiefly used in stately and superb structures. Callimachus took the hint of the capital of this column from the following remarkable circumstance, accidently passing the tomb of a young lady, he perceived a basket of toys, which had been left there by her nurse, covered with a tile, and placed over an acanthus root. As the leaves grew up, they encompassed the basket, till arriving at the tile, they met with an obstruction and bent downwards. Callimachus, struck with the object, set about imitating the figure; the vase of the capital he made to represent the basket, the abacus, the tile and the volutes, the bending leaves.

Yet not content with this utmost production of her own powers, Masonry held forth her torch and illumined the whole circle of arts and sciences. This gave rise to the Composite order, so named from being formed of parts of the other orders. Its capital is adorned with the two rows of leaves of the Corinthian, the volutes of the Ionic, and has the quarter-round of the Tuscan and Doric orders. Its column is ten diameters high; and its cornice has dentils or simple modillions. This order is chiefly used in structures where strength, elegance and beauty are displayed.

Painting and sculpture strained every nerve to decorate the buildings fair science has raised, while the curious hand designed the furniture and tapestry beautifying and adorning them with music, eloquence, poetry, temperance, fortitude, prudence, justice, virtue, honour, mercy, faith, hope and charity, plus many other Masonic emblems; but none shone with greater splendour than Brotherly Love, Relief and Truth.

At this point, it may come as no surprise to learn that the Second Emulation Lecture has just been presented in a necessarily foreshortened form. We were initially introduced to the science of Geometry, and its important role in the six-day creation of our earthly abode. Having placed mankind thereupon, the need for shelter brought about more elaborate forms of housing until wooden constructions were superseded by those of stone, and modern architecture consequently evolved.

Connections with Masonry have been frequently alluded to, and in conclusion, the lecture draws a Fellow Craft's attention to the letter 'G' denoting *God*. However, there is no doubt that when the 'G' was commonly employed back in eighteenth century Freemasonry, usually at the heart of a blazing star, it represented *Geometria*. This was many centuries before being employed by Grand Lodge to represent *God, the Grand Geometrician of the Universe* to whom it is claimed we must all submit; and whom we ought humbly to adore.

References:

Herbert Inman, *Emulation Working Explained* 1929 - Kessinger Publishing, Montana, USA

A. Lewis, *The Ritual for the Second Degree*, Lewis Masonic, Hersham 1972

Colin Dyer: *Emulation: A Ritual to Remember* Lewis Masonic, Hersham 1973

Harvey Lovewell, *Geometry and Masonry*, Grand Lodge of Queensland, Australia 2003

Graham Redman, *Emulation Working Today*, Lewis Masonic, Hersham 2007

CHAPTER TEN

RITUAL AND FREEMASONRY

RITUAL IS USUALLY defined as a prescribed order of performing rites or a procedure regularly followed. The familiarity with which someone engages in ritualistic behaviour reinforces the correctness of the procedure and brings comfort and security. The act of making a cup of tea in a certain way over and over again ensures that the result is predictably enjoyable every time. Change even the tiniest part of the ritual, for example a different shaped tea bag, and an element of doubt and suspicion arises, perhaps even a subconscious panic, 'Will it taste the same this time?'

The older one gets the more ritualised one's behaviour, elderly people often settle down in the same armchair with a favourite cup, placing it on the coffee table in precisely the same way at the same set times each day. The accidental breaking of the cup may throw the entire procedure into major crisis.

At a more extreme level, sufferers from Obsessive Compulsive Disorder need the ritual of perhaps washing the hands twenty times before allowing themselves even to partake of a cup of tea (Perhaps after washing the cup the same number of times too!) It would be fair to say that *ritual* preceded *language* in the area we call social interaction, and long before human beings enjoyed verbal forms of communication, they would have needed a kind of signing shorthand to indicate that perhaps a stranger or wild animal was approaching the cave, or that a baby's birth was imminent.

The repetitive setting of traps, digging of pits or lighting of fires would also have attracted ritualised participation, and the subsequent festive board, would most likely have been marked by offering the first cut of meat to the dominant male, who was no doubt careful to emphasise his privilege by signalling, if and when the subservient members of the tribe were allowed to partake of the hunting spoils. Bees, it is commonly known, communicate the finding of a new source of honey, by performing a ritual dance to indicate its distance and direction.

Many animals however use ritual as a form of self-preservation. When engaged in a fight, the vanquished male will often adopt a submissive pose or other ritualised behaviour, acknowledging the victor's superiority and thereby inviting him to end his aggression, secure in the knowledge that the weaker has no further interest in the contest. Curiously, humans also occasionally adopt this system.

Ritual provides a framework to organise events, we don't like chaos, we make lists so that we don't forget things we want to buy or do. Performing tasks in a set order, like for instance mending a car ensures that we don't finish the job with several strange nuts and bolts left over. Similarly, the morning ritual makes sure that we don't leave the house unshaven, and without our car-keys or money. Ritual is a form of mental checklist, which helps to prevent disasters and ensures a smooth running day.

Ritual assists our relationship with others; almost every family has its rituals. These might include eating together on certain days or phoning each other at set times. Outside the family, the ritual of shaking hands with strangers is an obvious advantage. It gives a clear message that we are aware of social etiquette, and enables the conversation to flow in an easy and relaxed manner. In former times, 'kowtowing' by prostrating oneself before an oriental dignitary, ensured that one's head remained firmly attached to the body.

Ritual is a formidable teaching tool. From the very earliest times, tribes would use ritual to ensure that its youngest members were able to join hunting parties, with the correct end of the spear facing the animal. When we repeat the mnemonic, 'Richard of York gained battles in vain' we are able to remember the colours of the rainbow with ease. In Military circles, similar repetitive phrases enable recruits to remember how to dismantle and clean their firearms. Chanting marching songs maintains a soldier's morale but also keeps him in step.

Ritual is a useful preparatory signal for what is to follow; the Greenwich Time signal will alert us to the impending radio news programme, similarly the *Eastenders* signature tune will speed us to the sofa for the next mind-numbing television episode. We would feel cheated if such signals were omitted and we were obliged to keep checking our watch. Finally, ritual enables us to abbreviate our lives in certain areas, so saving time for the things we love and enjoy. This includes a form of shorthand with our friends and family. For instance, down the pub, 'Another?' conveys the subtle message, 'It's your round really, but you've probably forgotten, so I guess I'll just have to get them in!' Similarly at home, 'one lump or two?' conveniently leaves out the word 'sugar'. The sending of text and cell phone messages is the very latest form of ritual abbreviation, which has evolved to allow the youth of today more time to spend our money.

Throughout history, ritual has interlocked with habit to reinforce social cohesion, at its simplest when Roman Legions marched into battle and at its most elaborate, at Coronations or State Openings of Parliament when the whole nation feels bound together by a carefully scripted and televised ceremony. Whenever a family or indeed a nation is beset with difficulties, ritual activity reinforces the bonds of kinship, for instance the placing of flowers at the scene of an accident, or on a larger scale the thousands placed outside Kensington Palace on the death of Princess Diana.

Perhaps it is in the area of religion that we see the clearest function of ritual, literally to signify that we are all '…singing from the same hymn book'. Whether it is the Catholic liturgy, Islamic worship or Buddhist chanting, a clear message of purposeful unification is reinforced among the gathered congregation. Three thousand years ago the Jewish people followed a predetermined pattern of worship, which prescribed every detail, from their sacrifices and apparel to the very priesthood itself.

The Hare Krishna movement today takes ritual to its extreme with its emphasis on repetitive chanting. The community is an indispensable part of Society. The Muezzin calls the Muslim faithful to prayer, Christian church bells chime, the Shofar is sounded, the University bell bids its tutors and students assemble and the Lodge invites members and Brothers of the Mystic Tie to share in a communal ceremony marked at its beginning and end by acknowledging the power and wisdom of the *Great Architect of the Universe*.

But, when does the ritual really begin at a Masonic meeting? Arguably it is long before the Master asks his Junior Warden the first care. Some might say that the opening ode is a symbolic affirmation of singing from that common hymnbook so vital to Lodge unity. Others may point to the Director of Ceremonies calling the Brethren to order, but surely it is the donning of the regular dark suit and sombre tie, the exchange of greetings with new arrivals and the pint in the bar that gives the earliest message that here is a club whose members are 'people like us', whose rules are clear, and whose environment is safe and secure.

When a newcomer wishes to participate in our assemblies, we unconsciously need to feel confident that he will 'fit in', that he poses no threat to our unity, that he might introduce others of his ilk to swell our numbers, the underlying motive being of course, to increase our kind by a regenerative process. It is for this reason that traditionally, societies have evolved initiation ceremonies like the bar mitzvahs, the rites of passage etc. etc. From Royalty to Gypsies, the purity of the bloodline is constantly being safeguarded, similarly, the quality of our candidates in Freemasonry.

So why is there so much ritual in our ceremonies? At the time when Freemasonry was purely operative, the ceremony for admitting an apprentice was essential to impress upon him the seriousness of his undertaking, to spend the next seven years learning the rudiments of the Craft. As this ritual was never written down, we can only guess its details. His honesty and dedication would be assured by reminding him of his obligations. An oath to that effect would most likely have been necessary. The reward for such commitment would be the receipt of a password, which would enable him to move about the site and gain access to his lodgings. As a safeguard to those privileges a further vow would be necessary, not to reveal the password, under pain of physical penalty. There would most likely be a further ceremony to mark the completion of his apprenticeship when another password would be communicated so that he could receive his wages, no doubt with even stronger penalties for revealing it.

With the passage of time, Lodges of operative stonemasons began to admit non-operatives to their ceremonies. These became more frequent and elaborate, and as the number of Lodges increased it is understandable that by natural wastage some eventually lost all their operatives. It is possible that the surviving members would seek to reinforce the value and meaning of their activities by using the symbolic nature of the stonemason's working tools as guidelines for moral and spiritual development, and by placing emphasis on the secrecy and uniqueness of its ceremonies. Masonic ritual ensures that every candidate enters Freemasonry on an equal basis 'poor and penniless' sharing the same experience, whatever their position or status outside the craft. This experience of shared ritual fosters a bond of faith and Brotherhood among all members of the Fraternity.

The fundamental objective of Masonic ritual is to forcibly impress its principles upon the candidate's mind, and to create in him a new nature. Its focus must always be on the instruction and improvement of the candidate. It should inspire him, offer him an emotionally satisfying experience, excite his imagination, and kindle his desire for further knowledge.

All ritual is repetitive in its nature. By regularly attending meetings, hearing the same words and observing the same perambulations reveals new insights and imparts new interpretations to them, Freemasonry is not just concerned with teaching morals, these are only a preparation for understanding its hidden mysteries. It is a spiritual science, and lessons of the spirit can only be conveyed in this manner, because although they are simultaneously taught to many, they can be understood only in proportion to the individual's level of development and preparation.

This science is universal and timeless. It teaches us to consolidate our faith in God, by incorporating the square of justice, the plumb-rule of uprightness, and the breadth of compasses to restrain our passions. Add to these the 24-inch gauge by which to divide our time into prayer, labour, and service to our fellow creatures and we can face our future without fear or regret.

The opening and closing of a Lodge are fully ritualised. The procedure ensures that everyone is in their proper place and understands their duty. The prayer guarantees that nothing takes place without remembering that His *All Seeing Eye* observes our every move. The alms collection confirms that charitable giving is '…one of the three great principles on which the Order is founded.' Even the voting takes place in a ritualised fashion, so that everyone is confident that it is properly conducted.

Then there are the Degrees, during which the candidate is ritually confronted by the Master and Wardens to show that he has been properly prepared and has been made aware of his new responsibilities once accepted. This he confirms on the Volume of the Sacred Law. An even more elaborate form of ritual occurs on evenings of Installation.

Why then are there so many different workings in Masonry? Some are rendered in song, others even in rhyming couplets, some are extremely casual and yet others are organised with military precision. How has this all come about? I am indebted to Worshipful Brother Colin Dyer, whose Prestonian Lecture in 1973 was entitled 'In Search of Ritual Uniformity' and attempted to examine the regulation and development of Craft Ritual Procedures since 1813.

In 1973, the *Book of Constitutions*, Rule 155 stated that:

> …the members present at any Lodge duly summoned have an undoubted right to regulate their own proceedings, provided they are consistent with the general law and regulations of the Craft.

Nowadays sadly there is no mention of ritual anywhere in the Book of Constitutions; the current craft ritual appertaining to the 'three degrees' dates from the union of the *Antients* and *Moderns* in 1813. Until that time there were considerable differences and much of the unification of ritual was the work of William Preston, after whom the familiar annual lectures have been named. In the early 1800's Preston's ritual was being taught at Lodges of Instruction in the form of Lectures, one for each degree.

After the unification, a special Lodge of Reconciliation was set up to amend and amalgamate the rituals in an attempt to bring about some uniformity of working. By 1819, Lodges of Instruction were firmly established, although these had to be sanctioned by the Master of an associated Lodge. There were plenty of rules and regulations which governed their setting up, but only the personal involvement of the Duke of Sussex, and his preoccupation with uniformity, managed to produce a common system of workings by the end of the 1830's, and this was mainly in the London area.

The Earl of Zetland succeeded the Duke as Grand Master in 1844. His achievements are readily acknowledged, but his attitude towards the ritual was much more relaxed. Masonic publications soon began to highlight the differences between those who wished to *embellish and innovate* and those who were in favour of the status quo. In fact in 1847 it was pointed out to the Earl that his proposal that *'free born'* should no longer apply and that his statement that all who were free should be eligible, was contrary to the lectures. His laconic reply was, 'Then the lectures must be altered.'

An important contribution towards the attempted standardisation of the ritual were the Public Nights, held by the Grand Steward's Lodge from the 1830s to the 50s, but attendances after that began to fall sharply, as by then many Lodges were already incorporating significant differences in their own rituals. Richard Carlisle printed one of the earliest Ritual Books in 1838. George Bradshaw, published another in 1851, from an address given at a Public House, similar to the one used by Carlisle, in order to avoid possible censure.

The most salient event in the diversification of the ritual happened in the 1870s. This was the relaxation of the total ban on the printing and publication of information on Masonic ritual. By 1874, John Hogg had published his guide to Emulation working, under the title: *The Perfect Ceremonies of Craft Masonry*. (As taught in the Emulation Lodge of Improvement at Freemasons' Hall since 1823) This was without any form of censure from on high, and a flood of printed material soon followed from anyone who wished to publicise their own particular system of ritual. Some sought to change the grammatical contents of established rituals, some wanted to include more religious references, and some simply tried to bring the ritual 'up-to-date'.

One famous publisher of Masonic ritual was George Claret, who unashamedly admitted that he altered successive editions by introducing his own variations and alternatives. The trouble was, and still is, the average Freemason depends on the written word and regards it as Gospel, without questioning its origins. Thereafter various workings found their way into print, including Oxford, Logic, West End, Complete,

Revised, Durham, Bottomley, Common Sense and Taylor's, not to mention Stability, Muggeridge, Kentish Antiquity and other private Lodge rituals. *M.M. Taylor's Handbook of Craft Freemasonry* was so named to avoid confusion with any other published Ritual Book. The 1908 edition claims that its chief merit is being:

> …up-to-date, having been compiled by several experienced brethren who have devoted a great number of years to the study and practice of the various ceremonies, and who have every reason to believe that this work will tend to bring about that which has been so much desired by Freemasons, viz. – 'Universal Working.'

Later in the 1900s saw the intervention by Provincial Grand Masters, many of whom felt that a standardised working should be adopted throughout the Province, so for example the Province of Sussex now only permits a modified version of 'Nigerian' working. The Grand Lodge has intervened on just two occasions, the first in 1963 to regulate the content of music in Ceremonies, and in 1964 to authorise an alternative version of the Obligation in respect of Masonic penalties. Since then certain Brethren have formed associations to promote particular workings, one of which is notably concerned with promoting Taylor's Ritual, but no attempt appears to have been made centrally from Grand Lodge to define a truly universal ritual.

Despite the many variations to be found among printed workings, a surprising amount of similarity still exists. It is as if certain landmarks are instinctively sacrosanct. W. Bro. Colin Dyer sees the fundamental practice of testing, obligating and entrusting a candidate as:

> A series of Ritual acts in a particular sequence: words are used as part of those Ritual acts in order to convey a particular sense and to emphasise a particular point and in certain cases certain specific words should be used, but the precise words may not, in every case be important in themselves. If every word were of such importance, then every slip in Lodge must be corrected or the Ceremony must be treated as not having been properly conducted and the Candidate must repeat it - which is nonsense. At the same time the true sense must be preserved or the Ceremonies would take on a different meaning as time went by.

Tinkering with the Ritual therefore, without a fundamental grasp of its historical and traditional context can do more harm than good. No doubt for that reason, the Board of General Purposes are probably reluctant to authorise a standard Craft Ritual and it is likely that the number of variations throughout the Masonic world will inevitably increase until perhaps a natural process of stabilisation occurs. How this might arise, one cannot be sure.

It is my personal view that just as in nature, ritualised behaviour evolves organically to meet ever-changing circumstances, so too will our Masonic ritual inevitably evolve, as Freemasonry meets the challenges of the twenty-first century. It is unlikely that consensus will promote one ritual over the rest, so the most likely outcome is that those who see their ritual as carved in stone could well suffer falling numbers and their Lodges might even be erased if they fail to adapt. The rituals, which survive this evolutionary process, may well plagiarise each other's word groupings until a form of Masonic *franglais* emerges.

The problem facing anyone who wishes to modernise the ritual, is maintaining the delicate balance between common usage of the language and the traditional landmarks, which have always been expressed in an *Antient* form. He must never lose sight of the purpose and meaning of the ceremonies. Indeed he must mark the candidate's 'rite of passage', in a manner that convinces the assembled Brethren that the candidate fully appreciates the seriousness of the steps he is taking and the solemnness of the oaths accompanying them. He must then distinguish between those paragraphs, which impress upon the candidate the reality of the occasion, and those, which are in danger of floating over his head like so much gobbledegook.

It is not just a case of simply removing the jargon, but looking at every section of the ritual, to identify its purpose, and to find the best way to express it within an integrated framework. The biggest danger is that of reducing the ritual to a pale and impoverished version, which may be viewed at best, sterile and at its worst, trite and meaningless.

What I have illustrated however, is an attempt to clarify the communication, without losing the seriousness of the moment, for whatever the wording, until Brother Inner Guard has ascertained the Tyler's presence by a few hard knocks, the Lodge will be completely unable to function. As for the rest of the ritual, perhaps one day someone will examine and evaluate it, as in this modest example.

Who knows, an enthusiastic brother may well be doing this as I speak. At the beginning of this chapter, we looked at the origins and applications of ritual. We then examined its progress through the years and discovered that despite the best intentions of dedicated ritualists, the inevitable march of progress has pulled our Masonic Rituals into various configurations, and it looks like the process is destined to continue.

However, looking at the results after two hundred years, it seems clear that with appropriate fidelity to our landmarks and traditions, Masonic Ritual has a solid future and is unlikely to be sacrificed lightly on the altar of progress. In concluding this brief look at the origins, and even more briefly, the future of Masonic ritual, we reach the point where formality ceases. The Brethren relax, hopefully with their curiosity about the subject satisfied. A look at the clock indicates that there are only so many minutes left before the Lodge is closed and they can soon regroup in the bar, their thirst for knowledge assuaged and their ritual thirst for liquid refreshment about to be gratified.

CHAPTER ELEVEN

WHO WAS ADONIRAM?

ACCORDING TO EDGAR Jones of the *Quatuor Coronati* Correspondence Circle:

> Not the least of the mysteries which perplex the Freemason is the sudden appearance in the Installation Ceremony of a hitherto unknown figure, Adoniram, whose abrupt elevation from total obscurity to a position of pre-eminence is quite unexplained. Masons asked about this phenomenon seem to have been in the main content to accept it without question or comment, but occasions arise when some explanation is sought.

In Mackey's *Lexicon of Freemasonry*, Adoniram plays an important part in the Masonic system, especially in advanced degrees. Any Mark Master Mason will remember his name being mentioned whenever a Mark Lodge is opened. The Inner Workings of a Mark Installation ceremony also attributes to Adoniram the peculiar signs of a Mark Master. But in Craft his appearance is mainly confined to providing Lebanese timber for the Temple's construction. The legends and traditions which connect him with that superb edifice derive their support from a single passage in the First Book of Kings, verses 12-14:

> And the LORD gave Solomon wisdom, as he promised him: and there was peace between Hiram King of Tyre and Solomon; and they two made a league together. And King Solomon raised a levy out of all Israel; and the levy was thirty thousand men. And he sent them to Lebanon, ten thousand a month by courses: a month they were in Lebanon, and two months at home: and Adoniram was over the levy.

From this brief statement some Freemasons have formed the theory, that Adoniram was the principle architect of the Temple; while others, designating this important office to Hiram Abif, nevertheless believe that Adoniram played an important part in its construction. He has been called 'The first of the Fellow Crafts' and is said in one tradition to have been Hiram Abif's brother-in-law, Hiram Abif having demanded the hand of Adoniram's sister in marriage; and that the nuptials were honoured by the Kings of Israel and Tyre with a public celebration.

However, in a 336 page thorough examination of *The Secrets of Solomon's Temple* by Kevin Gest, devoted to discovering the roots of Freemasonry, his only mention of Adoniram is the previous biblical quotation from the First Book of Kings, nothing else! However, this author took twelve years of persistent enquiry and deliberation, before committing his findings to print. He thoroughly examined all the theories around the construction of great religious buildings and challenged many of the fundamental impressions we may have inherited from previous generations, regarding the fables of King Solomon and his revered Temple. How odd then, that the actual appearance of Adoniram was so clearly dismissed by him as irrelevant.

By contrast, Mackenzie's *Royal Masonic Cyclopedia* does suggest that with a name meaning 'High Lord', Adoniram was in fact the principal treasurer of King Solomon, and the chief overseer of the 30,000 brethren sent to fell timber in the forests of Lebanon. Others claim that Adoniram and Hiram Abif were one and the same person, though one being the spiritual reincarnation of the other.

Researchers often question the juxtaposition of the title Adon (Lord) with that of Hiram, even if the intention of the legend's compilers was to focus equal attention on the two main participants in Masonic ceremony. It may seem rather illogical, but there is no known mythology, which develops according to a strict logical pattern. Mythologies frequently attempt to reconcile differing schools of thought through fusing's, borrowings and symbolic overlapping of apparently contradictory elements.

However, the first occurrence of Adoniram in the Bible is in the Second Book of Samuel, Chapter twenty, verse twenty-four, where, in the abbreviated form of his name; Adoram, he is identified as chief collector of taxes. Later in Kings 1, Chapter four, verse six, we find him fulfilling the identical function in Solomon's household, 'Adoniram the son of Abda was over the tribute.' Finally, we find Adoniram still occupying the same position in the household of King Rehoboam, Solomon's successor. Commentators have been unable to determine whether the tax-receiver under David, under Solomon, and under Rehoboam were one and the same person, there seems to be no room for doubt; as Kitto says:

> …it appears very unlikely that even two persons of the same name should successively bear the same office, in an age when no example occurs of the father's name being given to his son.

John Eitto in his *Cyclopedia of Biblical Literature* points out that not more than forty-seven years elapse between the first and last mention of the Adoniram who was '…over the tribute', that is a tax collector, and as this is not too long for one life and as the person who held the office in the beginning of Rehoboam's reign had served in it long enough to make himself odious to the people, it appears, on the whole, most likely that one and the same person is intended throughout.

In his book, *Who was Hiram Abif?* John Sebastian Ward majors on the '…death and resurrection' ceremonies of tribes in Africa, Australia and North America. In fact, that very theme is also symbolised in fertility ceremonies around the world, where fresh growth appears from planted seeds. Indeed, an 'ear of corn near to a fall of water' plays an important part in the Second Degree ceremony.

While if we move on to the Third Degree, the symbolism of 'death and resurrection' could not be more graphically represented. Indeed the 'five points of fellowship' on which the body of our Master Hiram was raised could hardly be less symbolic of resurrection. And, to raise a dead body to such a vertical position (given the problems of rigor mortis and putrification) could only have been symbolic, if attempted at all. In real life the discovery of a body, would surely have meant simply covering it up again tidily and leaving a marker (like for example a sprig of Acacia) so that full recovery at a later date could be made by King Solomon's officials.

It will probably now come as some surprise then that during the very next Craft ceremony a Master Mason may experience, his Installation the unexplained appearance of someone called Adoniram not only deserves the immediate approval of King Solomon, but he is regarded so highly that he is even prevented from kneeling. Surely a personality of such obvious importance would merit at least a single mention somewhere in the earlier accounts of the Temple construction?

If not, then why not? For some kind of answer to that question, we must inevitably turn to the very symbolism, which is at the heart of Freemasonry. A dagger presented to the naked breast, to imply that should a candidate rush forward 'He would have been an accessory to his own death by stabbing'. And a cable-tow with a running noose about his neck, to render any attempt at retreat '…equally fatal'.

The symbolic relevance of the Installation ceremony should now become obvious, for what is Freemasonry if it is not about death and resurrection, the death of the old ego and the rebirth of the new assisted by Masonic line and rule? The Installation ceremony carries the parallel one stage further. What could be more symbolic than the annual death of the old Master and the installation of his replacement, a graphic enactment of the Adonis mystery and a demonstrable return to a practice once highly valued by traditionalists? So if we cannot or will not appreciate the intended symbolism, the fault lies with us rather than in the compiler's intentions; or perhaps more accurately, in our education, which has virtually eradicated the building blocks of a mythical culture which once transcended the world's artificial boundaries.

Was Hiram Abif, in fact the same person as Adoniram? At first glance it doesn't appear very likely that the enormously skilled craftsman of Masonic legend, and the principal architect of the Temple, could be identical to the Biblical *Adoram* or Adoniram, the efficient and reliable civil servant who was either tax-collector or master of the labour gangs, or indeed both. It seems impossible to believe that the Masonic Hiram Abif was slain 'just before the completion of King Solomon's Temple', while the trusted civil servant, Adoniram was allegedly still very much alive during the reign of King Solomon's successor Rehoboam.

How can we explain then, that the Adoniram, whom King Solomon beckoned towards him, when visiting the newly completed Temple, could be on an equal footing with Hiram Abif? There are just two possibilities. The first is that Hiram, was indeed, a generic title given to the principal architect, just as the title of Pharaoh was awarded to the ruler of the Two Kingdoms and similarly Minos of Crete.

It would then seem incongruous that the murdered Hiram Abif's successor, who appears out of nowhere as a shadowy figure, then promptly disappears again, is awarded the honour of being given the title of *Adon* (Lord), which was never bestowed upon Hiram Abif, the 'Son of the Widow'. Perhaps the obvious conclusion is that the beckoned Adoniram, who was about to kneel in token of humility before his King, was not actually a physical presence but some kind of mystical reincarnation of the Principal Architect, now dead and buried.

Before we discount this possibility, perhaps we should consider that Hiram Abif, according to Masonic legend, was killed by three workmen just at the completion of King Solomon's magnificent temple. This may perhaps have its roots in Jewish legend that while all the workmen were killed to prevent them building another temple devoted to idolatry, the Principle Architect was raised to heaven like Enoch. Indeed, having been '...reinterred as near to the Sanctum Sanctorum as the Israelitish law would permit', Hiram's spiritual reincarnation would have been possible. Of course, one argument against this theory is that while we can accept that King Solomon was privileged to enjoy close and even physical contact with his dead servant.

On the other hand it was not suggested on this occasion that those accompanying the King (including the Queen of Sheba) were allowed the privilege of actually seeing Hiram, though a few eyebrows must have been raised by watching their King raise an invisible body from the kneeling position. The fact that there was not a single word of reply from Adoniram may however give a little more credence to this hypothesis. So what do we know about the compilers of the ceremony of Installation?

Back in 1827, the Earl of Zetland, at that time Deputy Grand Master, was charged with forming a 'Special Committee' on the orders of the Grand Master, His Royal Highness the Duke of Sussex, to '...draw up, revise, arrange or rearrange' the Installation Ceremony. On February 6th 1827, the Duke, having approved the ceremonial changes, issued a Warrant, authorising ten 'trusty and well-beloved Brothers' (these included the Grand Secretary, the Grand Registrar, and the Masters of seven senior Lodges) to promulgate them. That same year, according to the Grand Lodge Proceedings for 6th June:

> The Most Worshipful Grand Master stated that finding there was much diversity in the Ceremonial of the Installation of Masters of Lodges, and feeling it to be most desirable that uniformity should exist, His Royal Highness had deemed it expedient to issue a Warrant to certain intelligent others, directing them ... to hold meetings for the purpose of promulgating and giving instructions in this important ceremony that conformity might be produced.

Scholars have in fact detected no appearance of Adoniram prior to 1827. Neither was any trace of the story of Solomon's inspection of the Temple found in any text before that date. It follows that these additions must therefore have been included following the deliberations of the Select Committee. If such an important ceremony as the Installation Ceremony could have been reviewed in 1827, on the instruction of the highest Masonic authority, in order to eradicate many differing interpretations, thereby standardising the ceremony for all time, it must have been achieved with meticulous thought given to every detail.

The significance of Solomon's inspection of the Temple and his encounter with Adoniram must indicate more than just a chance encounter with an unidentifiable stonemason. It is inconceivable that the compilers had forgotten that Hiram Abif was killed earlier and buried. There must have been strong and consistent reasoning, involving death and resurrection, which made sense to each of them and must now make sense to us through the teachings of the New Testament.

For in the Gospel of St. John, Chapter 20, verses 17-19, the risen Jesus said to Mary Magdalene:

> Touch me not; for I am not yet ascended to my father: but go to my Brethren and say to them, I ascend unto my Father and your Father; and to my God, and your God. Mary Magdalene came and told the disciples that she had seen the Lord, and that he had spoken these things unto her. Then the same day at evening, being the first day of the week, when the doors were shut, where the disciples were assembled for fear of the Jews, came Jesus and stood in the midst, and saith unto them - Peace be unto you.

At the beginning of this paper, we encountered two separate icons of Masonic history, Hiram Abif and Adoniram, with their apparently separate involvement in the construction of King Solomon's Temple. Before long we learned that 'death and resurrection' were iconic symbols of various primitive societies, and that such symbolism was readily incorporated into Masonic ritual, especially at the behest of the Duke of Sussex in 1827.

The ceremony of Installation, representing the demise of one Worshipful Master and the advent of his successor, can only serve to underline the importance of symbolism in this our unique order, whose roots are buried deeper than the 'Age of Reason'. When the Royal Party had completed their inspection of King Solomon's Temple and were about to retire, Adoniram in token of humility saluted the King three times as if to say, 'Think of where I came from - death!'

References:

The Holy Bible, British & Foreign Bible Society, Glasgow 1957

A.G. Mackey, *Lexicon of Freemasonry*, Griffin, Bohn Co, London 1861

K.R.H. Mackenzie, *The Royal Masonic Cyclopedia*, John Hogg, London 1878

J.S.M. Ward, *Who was Hiram Abif?*, Baskerville Press, London 1925

Quatuor Coronati No. 108, Butler & Tanner, Frome & London 1990

K. L. Gest, *The Secrets of Solomon's Temple*, Lewis Masonic, Hersham 2007

CHAPTER TWELVE

HOGARTH'S 'NIGHT'

Hogarth's 'Night'
(Hogarth's Works, *c.1881, author's collection*)

WHAT IS A DRUNKEN Freemason doing in a picture by William Hogarth? Why do we find it exhibited in many Masonic buildings? Looking more closely, there seems to be a lot of chaos. What is the overturned coach about? Why the fires and fireworks? Surely this can't represent Guy Fawkes Night? After all, not many people seem to be enjoying themselves, least of all the Freemason, who is receiving the contents of a chamber pot on his head.

Not long ago I bought a selection of prints by Hogarth, including 'Night', but there were also unexpected bonuses of 'The Rake's Progress', and 'The Harlot's Progress' but sadly, despite his knowledge of the 'hidden mysteries of nature and science' a copy of the 'Fellow Craft's Progress' was nowhere to be seen.

'Night' was the final offering in a set describing the four times of the day, the other three being predictably, 'Morning', 'Noon' and 'Evening', each being a kind of social commentary equivalent to the pages of today's *Daily Mail*. For instance, 'Morning' is set in Covent Garden Market at eight o'clock, close by St Paul's Church and shows a variety of well-known people going about their business. In one corner a raucous disturbance is observed taking place among the customers of King's Coffee House, with sticks, cudgels and swords being waved about in anger. This appears to be recording events reported in a popular publication of the time.

Apparently the coffee house proprietor, Mrs Mary King was arrested and taken to court where she received the following sentence for keeping a disorderly house, '…to pay a fine of £200, to suffer three month's imprisonment, to find good security for her good behaviour for three years, and to remain in prison till the fine be paid.' As it was impossible for her to carry on her former business, as soon as she had completed her prison sentence, she retired with her savings, built three houses on Haverstock Hill, near Hampstead, and died in one of them in 1747. The inspiration for that picture probably came while Hogarth was taking coffee, just a stone's throw away from Mary King's Coffee House, in the nearby Bedford Coffee House in Covent Garden's Piazza, where he would regularly converse with his friends, John and Henry Fielding, the playwright Oliver Goldsmith and the actor David Garrick.

The patrons of Coffee Houses had to follow strict rules of conduct. According to the *Rules and Orders of the Coffee House* all men were equal and none need give up his seat to a 'finer' man. Anyone heard swearing was obliged to pay a forfeit of twelve pence and those caught quarrelling had to buy everyone involved a coffee. Furthermore, religion and politics were forbidden subjects, as the rules stated: 'Sacred things' must be excluded from conversation and the patrons could neither '…profane Scripture, nor saucily wrong Affairs of State with an irreverent tongue'.

The Rules and Orders just mentioned would hardly seem out of place in a Masonic Hall today, especially with Hogarth's picture of 'Night' hanging nearby. After all, who exactly was that drunken Freemason depicted staggering along the road? Which road? And what was he doing there in the first place? Mind you, I was surprised to discover that many prints in general circulation and even those on the Internet appear to have been printed back to front, or as you might say, 'mirror-images'.

The original print engraved by Charles Spooner is full of clues, but the back-to-front images seem to be devoid of any written details, like for instance the name on the side of the overturned stagecoach, the Salisbury Flying Coach, the nearby Barbershop sign 'Shaving, Bleeding, Teeth Drawing', and the 'Brothel' sign next to the Earl of Cardigan pub. Since the lettering on all of these would otherwise be back to front it would appear that they have been somehow erased from those prints.

Surely, these mirror images can't have been reproduced so as to avoid copyright problems, particularly in view of the fact that in his early years as an engraver Hogarth found that one of his first pictures to be sold, 'The Harlot's Progress' was being so frequently copied, that in 1735, he and a fellow art-student successfully petitioned parliament to tighten the laws on copyright.

The son of Richard Hogarth, a poor Latin teacher, William was born in London on November 10th 1697. His father's name was originally Hogard, which was derived from Hogherd. His wife persuaded him to change it to Hogarth, so that William would not have to bear a name generally associated with keeping pigs. As he grew up, William found that he had a good eye and was particularly fond of drawing. As he freely admitted:

> An early access to a neighbouring painter drew my attention from play; and I was, at every possible opportunity, employed in making drawings. I picked up an acquaintance of the same turn, and soon learnt to draw the alphabet with great correctness. My exercises, when at school, were more remarkable for the ornaments, which adorned them, than for the exercises themselves. In the former, I soon found that blockheads with better memories could much surpass me; but for the latter I was particularly distinguished.
>
> I thought it still more unlikely that by pursuing the common method, and copying old drawings, I could ever attain the power of making new designs, which was my first and greatest ambition. I therefore endeavoured to apply myself to the exercise of a sort of technical memory; and by repeating in my own mind the parts of which objects were composed, I could by degrees combine and put them down with my pencil. Thus, with all the drawbacks which resulted from the circumstances I have mentioned, I had one material advantage over my competitor... the early habit I thus acquired of retaining in my mind's eye, without coldly copying it on the spot, whatever I intended to imitate.

Hogarth's technical ability was soon in evidence, when he became apprenticed to a silver-plate engraver. He was subsequently accepted into the art school in St. Martin's Lane, where he studied life drawing, a skill that subsequently enabled him to portray the human form in all its character and raw emotions, but it was while still an apprentice that he began to develop a special talent for caricature.

One day, he was slaking his thirst at a local pub, in the company of a few friends, when a fight broke out and one of the participants, having no other weapon, brought his beer mug crashing down on his opponent's head with such force that it cracked open his skull. Hogarth, observing the bleeding man with such an expression of incredulity upon his face, took out his pencil and in less than a minute produced an exaggerated image of the unfortunate victim. This single event was to determine the whole course of Hogarth's future, to predate Charles Dickens as a social commentator.

William Hogarth's future fame was to lie in his observational skills and a draftsman's special ability to mock and satirise those in society, whom he held in contempt. For instance, in his later years William Hogarth produced satirical anti-war posters called 'The Times'. Hogarth published them in support of the minority who opposed the Seven Years War, including King George III and his chief advisor Lord Bute. William Pitt, who was Bute's opponent and leader of the Commons, supported the war and the economic benefits from the exploitation of British Colonies. Hogarth retaliated by depicting Pitt marching on stilts to fan the fires of war, while an Officer of the King was shown trying to extinguish them.

The Lord Mayor of London, William Beckford, himself a Pitt supporter, who had amassed a fortune from Jamaican tobacco and sugar plantations, was also shown in a doorway, pointing to a signboard advertising a naked Indian and reading Alive from America. This work upset quite a few M.P.s and one of the country's leading politicians, John Wilkes launched a vicious attack on Hogarth in his newspaper, The North Briton. Hogarth retaliated by publishing a caricature of the M.P., which he entitled 'John Wilkes Esquire'. Hogarth drew his adversary wearing a horn-like wig and holding his symbolic cap of liberty in such a way as to appear as if he were making a halo for himself.

Hogarth's 'Liberty'
(Hogarth's Works, *c.1881, author's collection*)

Hogarth suffered fools badly and was prone to fits of rage if criticised. Affability was apparently not one of his principal virtues and he would often find himself sent to Coventry in social circles for some caustic remark or cynical observation. Today such anti-social behaviour, combined with his exceptional graphic skills are the kind of symptoms, which could lead psychologists to conclude that Hogarth's apparent lack of social skills were probably the result of mild autism.

His marriage in 1730 to Jane, the only daughter of Sir James Thornhill, Fellow of the Royal Society and Past Senior Grand Warden, was problematical from the start. His bride-to-be was only eighteen years old, and her father objected to the match from the outset, regarding Hogarth as a cradle-snatcher. He was also intolerant of Hogarth's impecunious circumstances and his less than favourable reputation.

Despite such animosity, Hogarth apparently managed to preserve his marriage and at the same time develop his talents, so that by 1733 his illustrations were much in demand and his star was in the ascendant. However, his success did not prevent him being envious of others who rose to fame and popularity, such as Sir Joshua Reynolds, whose achievements he denigrated whenever possible, but there were just a few who claimed after his death that, '…he was liberal, hospitable, and the most punctual of paymasters, so that in spite of the emoluments his works had procured to him, he left a considerable fortune to his widow.'

By 1720 Hogarth is believed to have set up his own engraving business, designing and producing illustrations for booksellers. Many of his illustrations particularly that of 'Gin Lane' are still widely reproduced today. It was first circulated in 1751, the year in which a Gin Act was passed in Parliament that finally established control over the distribution of the destructive spirit.

Hogarth's 'Gin Lane' (Hogarth's Works, *c.1881, author's collection*)

At that time, gin was cheap, and alcoholism was rampant. In this graphic picture the central drunken character is portrayed as a negligent mother, oblivious of the potential danger to her child. He includes just the pawnbroker, distiller, and funeral parlour as the only sturdy buildings in a disintegrating landscape of suicide, poverty and degradation. By that time however, the foundations of Freemasonry and moral fortitude had been firmly established across British society.

So we must now turn to Hogarth's Masonic connections, and those aspects, which will be of special interest to the Brethren here today. We begin by outlining the influences of Freemasonry, which resulted in his producing the special picture which occupies our attention and which has aroused so much curiosity among future Brethren. By the age of 33, Hogarth was listed by Grand Lodge as being a member of a Lodge, which met at the Hand and Apple Tree, Little Queen Street, London.

His Masonic career progressed as far as becoming a Grand Steward, for according to Grand Lodge minutes on March 30th 1734:

> Then the twelve present Stewards were called up, and were thanked for the care they had taken in providing such an elegant entertainment for the Society, and at the same time, their healths were drank and each Steward was required to name his successor for the following year.

Hogarth's was the eighth name to be mentioned on the very same meeting, that the 20th Earl of Crawford succeeded the Right Honourable James Earl of Strathmore as Grand Master. Hogarth later designed the Grand Steward's Jewel for the Grand Lodge of England.

In 1736, Hogarth published a caricature of the past Grand Master, Dr John Theophilus Desaguliers, in his satirical representation, which was entitled: 'The Sleeping Congregation'. Hogarth also published a portrait of Martin Folkes, who had been Deputy Grand Master in 1724. Other famous Freemasons depicted by Hogarth include, Frederick the Prince of Wales, Charles Lennox, the Duke of Richmond, James Anderson, Anthony Sayer, Sir Robert Walpole and Richard 'Beau' Nash. But it is Hogarth's preoccupation with Sir Thomas de Veil (1684-1746), which is of particular interest to us today. Apparently, among the members of Hogarth's Lodge we find a Thomas Veal listed, and there are some who are convinced that Thomas Veal and Sir Thomas de Veil are really one and the same person.

Let's examine the evidence long before Hogarth was born, the streets of London were a dangerous place for anyone of substance or affluence. Muggings and theft were the order of the day, and the City of London Council brought in many acts, which attempted to improve the policing of the Capital. For instance the 1663 Night Watch Act stipulated that a Constable's authority extended to the entire City and not just his own patch. It also increased the number of Watchmen who could then call upon any Constable to assist in the apprehension of a wrongdoer.

Until the middle of the eighteenth century local unpaid Justices of the Peace dispensed summary justice. This system was open to corruption, with J.P.s earning fees for licensing public houses and being remunerated for every criminal they convicted. The origins of a professional Magistrate's Bench owes its existence to Sir Thomas de Veil. He was a Huguenot, a soldier who leased premises in Bow Street, owned by the Duke of Bedford, at £30 per year, which he converted into a proper court for his work as a Middlesex Justice.

In 1735, Sir Thomas became the first recipient of a Royal Warrant, which was granted by King George II. To this day every District Judge holds office by virtue of having been granted a Royal Warrant. Sir Thomas de Veil's Bow Street premises were later used by Hogarth's friend, Henry Fielding, who set up a cohort of paid 'Thief-takers' who eventually became known as the 'Bow Street Runners'. The runners were in fact private detectives paid for trying to solve crimes and capture and help to convict known criminals. They were instantly dismissed if there was any suspicion that they were operating outside the law or on their own. Later of course came Sir Robert Peel, whose 'Peelers' or 'Bobbies' would evolve into the Metropolitan Police Force.

Now let us return to William Hogarth and 'Night'. This engraving was, as I have already said, the last to be published in a set of four, each one satirising 'The Four Times of the Day'. They were originally offered for sale for five shillings each. 'Night' was actually dated March 25th 1738 and this date can be confirmed by the presence of oak leaves in the barber's sign and in the hat worn by two of the men in the picture. The oak leaves are believed to represent the forthcoming anniversary on May 29th of the restoration of King Charles II to the English throne.

The night time scene almost certainly depicts Hartshorn Lane, Charing Cross, which was later known as Northumberland Street (currently Northumberland Avenue) which was eventually widened and which opens onto Trafalgar Square. Artistic license has obviously been employed in depicting the equestrian statue of King Charles I, which would not normally have been viewed as such from this perspective. The inclusion of the statue obviously reinforces the connection with his successor, Charles II.

The scene includes on the one side the Rummer Tavern and on the other the Cardigan's Head, both next to notorious brothels, the signs 'Bagnio' and 'New Bagnio' above clearly stating the building's purpose. Apparently, the only connection between the Rummer Tavern and Freemasonry is that a Lodge constituted 18th August 1732 met there briefly until 1733. The tavern opposite, The Earl of Cardigan's Head was believed to be the venue for the Union French Lodge, constituted 17th August 1732. Another Lodge, which was constituted 15th April 1728, also held its meetings there from 1739-1742.

Let us now consider the Salisbury Coach, which has just picked up passengers from the taverns and has overturned by driving through a bonfire. Its passengers are doubly disturbed by the firebrand, doubtless thrown into its open window by a local urchin. This is said to be a burlesque on a right honourable peer of the realm, who was prone to driving his carriage recklessly about the countryside over hedges and into ditches and rivers, often walking away and leaving the servants to salvage the carriage themselves.

Opposite the coach we see a wounded Freemason, looking as though he has had one too many and is in need of support to find his way home. J. Nichols in his work, *'Biographical Anecdotes of William Hogarth'* claims that '…in Night, the drunken Freemason has been supposed to be Sir Thomas de Veil; but Sir John Hawkins assures me, it is not in the least like him' Others apparently differ and a contemporary portrait of him certainly bears a remarkable likeness.

The Square suspended from the Freemason's neck would indicate that he is either a Reigning or Past Master. His long apron might suggest a practical use behind the bar, or simply serve to remind us that today's aprons are much more decorative than functional. The sword and key carried by his companion suggests that he was probably the Tyler, and the mark on his forehead suggests that he may have just taken his duties seriously to '…keep off all Cowans and intruders to Masonry'. In fact some believe he represents the Grand Tyler, Brother Andrew Montgomery. However, we presume the lamp being carried was merely to guide the pair of them home, rather than to suggest 'darkness visible'.

The indignant prostitute portrayed in the window above is seen showing her contempt for Sir Thomas by showering him with the contents of her chamber pot. In February 1738, Sir Thomas de Veil succeeded Horace Walpole as Inspector General of Imports and Exports, a function today of the Customs and Excise Department.

Hogarth's lampooning of Sir Thomas as a drunken sot, too inebriated to find his own way home without assistance, hints at some measure of hypocrisy in the Magistrate's harsh sentencing of drunkards, when he was more than fond of a tipple himself. He was so punitive with those who sold spirits, particularly gin, that a local villain assembled a gang with the intention of destroying Sir Thomas's house and taking their revenge on two 'informers' who were lodged inside. The ringleader was eventually caught and tried for the offence but subsequently acquitted on the grounds of insanity.

Just below the familiar striped barbershop pole (the red and white juxtaposed to represent the shaving cream and blood-letting) we can see the barber through the window, shaving a customer. While on the bench outside we can see six shallow cups, believed to contain the blood let from previous customers. Included in the picture, underneath the barber's bench are some destitute children sleeping together for warmth and protection while another looks as though on close inspection that he is attempting to light a cigarette from the firebrand he is holding, although it is just possible he is only blowing it into more life.

Nearby, the publican is seen apparently watering down his beer, a practice that has long endured, unless of course he is returning the ullage from beneath the barrels inside the tavern. Some people suggest that he is actually topping-up the barrel with Gin or Burgundy. In the background we can observe a horse drawing a cart full of household possessions, doubtless to prevent the bailiffs from taking possession of them. Even further in the distance we can see flames lighting up the night sky from some local building, which has somehow caught fire.

Finally we see two foreground figures, generally agreed to be '…Free and Accepted Masons', having just left the meeting and coming to assist the terrified occupants of the overturned coach. One carries a wooden sword, probably the Inner Guard and the other, possibly the Junior Deacon, has a mop in his hand, suggesting that his duties could have included washing off the tracing board, drawn with chalk on the floor of the room nearby used by the Lodge.

It is believed that this part of the picture also has a satirical meaning, the steel hanging from his belt would normally be used by a butcher to sharpen his knives, and by playing on the word *'Veal'* alludes to the name De Veil; finally and conclusively proving to some observers that the main character in the engraving was specifically drawn to represent none other than Sir Thomas De Veil.

The name De Veil, which can also be pronounced 'Devil', may well have inspired the whole concept and depiction of 'Night', under cover of which the controls normally concealing disorder, confusion and violence are no longer present, a time of the day when the Devil rides, evil abounds and no one is safe. The play on the main character's name may therefore have added a sinister dimension to the work, in that the scene, with its abundant fires, the dangerous bonfire, the firebrand thrown into the Salisbury Coach, the boy's own firebrand, the burning building in the background, added to which the blood on the table, and the chaos inside an overturned carriage, all combine to suggest some kind of living hell.

The whole night-time scenario would appear to be Hogarth's view of disorder and depravity, comically depicted in a moment of stasis. Just as episodes of television soap operas such as *Eastenders* encapsulate far more drama and activity than might normally occur within half an hour of reality. So the artist creates a visual amalgam, alluding to an overflowing and constantly changing world in one snapshot image, conveniently captured at a fixed moment in time. William Hogarth has left us a fascinating glimpse of eighteenth century society.

His dramatic depiction of 'Night' prevents us from viewing his characters through the historian's rose-tinted glasses, and whereas the writings of Charles Dickens ensured that the poverty and injustice of his day were graphically described and preserved for posterity, so Hogarth's poignant caricatures help us to remember that by night or by day we cannot forget that there are always those less fortunate than ourselves, '… and cheerfully embrace the opportunity of practicing towards them that quality we now admire.'

References:

R. F. Gould, *The History of Freemasonry*, 1886

Anon, *The Works of Hogarth*, J. Dicks, London, c.1875

John Nichols, *Biographical Anecdotes of William Hogarth*, J. Nichols, London, 1785G.W. Speth, *Ars Quatuor Coronati* Vol. 1 p.116, Quatuor Coronati, London 1888

J. Pelzer and L. Pelzer (October 1982) 'Coffee Houses of Augustan London', *History Today*: 40–47.

'Night' *William Hogarth (1697-1764)*

INDEX